Touch Me There!

About the Author

Originally from Iceland, sexologist and relationship expert Dr. Yvonne Fulbright has a master's degree in human sexuality education from the University of Pennsylvania and received her Ph.D. in international community health, with a focus in sexual health, from New York University. She is the author of *The Hot Guide to Safer Sex, Touch Me There! A Hands-On Guide to Your Orgasmic Hot Spots,* and *Sex with Your Ex & 69 Other Things You Should Never Do.* Through her books, workshops, seminars, and consulting, Dr. Fulbright has established herself as a leading contemporary sexuality expert. She has appeared on CNN's *Paula Zahn NOW* and NBC's *Today* show, and her work has been reviewed or featured in *USA Today, The New York Times, Men's Health UK,* and *Cosmopolitan.*

Yvonne is a member of the American Association of Sex Educators, Counselors, and Therapists (AASECT) and the Society for the Scientific Study of Sexuality (SSSS), and continues to develop her "sexpertise" as an adjunct professor of human sexuality at Argosy University and as co-host of *Sex Files* on the Sirius Maxim Channel 108. In 2004 she founded Sexuality Source, a communications and consulting organization specializing in sex, sexual health, and relationships. For more information about her projects, visit www.sexualitysource.com.

Other titles in the Positively Sexual series

Sex Tips & Tales from Women Who Dare *edited by* Jo-Anne Baker

Extended Massive Orgasm *by* Steve Bodansky, Ph.D., and Vera Bodansky, Ph.D.

The Illustrated Guide to Extended Massive Orgasm
by Steve Bodansky, Ph.D., and Vera Bodansky, Ph.D.

To Bed or Not to Bed *by* Vera Bodansky, Ph.D., and Steve Bodansky, Ph.D.

Women's Sexual Passages *by* Elisabeth Davis

Sensual Sex *by* Beverly Engel, MFCC

The Hot Guide to Safer Sex *by* Yvonne Fulbright, M.S.Ed.

Touch Me There! *by* Yvonne Fulbright, M.S.Ed.

Making Love Better Than Ever *by* Barbara Keesling, Ph.D.

Rx Sex *by* Barbara Keesling, Ph.D.

Sexual Healing *by* Barbara Keesling, Ph.D.

Sexual Pleasure *by* Barbara Keesling, Ph.D.

Simultaneous Orgasm *by* Michael Riskin, Ph.D., and Anita Banker-Riskin, M.A.

Tantric Sex for Women *by* Christa Schulte

Female Ejaculation and the G-Spot *by* Deborah Sundahl

Ordering

Trade bookstores in the U.S. and Canada please contact
Publishers Group West
1700 Fourth Street, Berkeley CA 94710
Phone: (800) 788-3123   Fax: (800) 351-5073

For bulk orders please contact
Special Sales
Hunter House Inc., PO Box 2914, Alameda CA 94501-0914
Phone: (510) 899-5041   Fax: (510) 865-4295
E-mail: sales@hunterhouse.com

Individuals can order our books by calling **(800) 266-5592**
or from our website at **www.hunterhouse.com**

touch me there!

**A HANDS-ON GUIDE
TO YOUR ORGASMIC
HOT SPOTS**

Yvonne K. Fulbright, Ph.D.

Hunter House PUBLISHERS

Hunter House Inc., Publishers
PO Box 2914
Alameda CA 94501-0914

Library of Congress Cataloging-in-Publication Data
Fulbright, Yvonne K.
Touch me there! : a hands-on guide to your orgasmic hot spots /
Yvonne K. Fulbright. — 1st ed.
p. cm. — (Positively sexual series)
Includes bibliographical references and index.
ISBN-13: 978-0-89793-488-6 (pbk.)
ISBN-13: 978-0-89793-549-4 (ebook)
1. Sex instruction—Popular works. 2. Sex—Popular works. I. Title.
HQ31.F87 2007
613.9'6—dc22   2006035820

Project Credits

Cover Design	Brian Dittmar Graphic Design
Book Production	John McKercher
Anatomical illustrations	Lisa Kroin
All other illustrations	Alexis McQuilkin
Models	Paula D. Atkinson and Gregory Stuart
Photographer	Charles G. Fulbright
Copy Editor	Kelley Blewster
Proofreader	John David Marion
Indexer	Yvonne K. Fulbright
Acquisitions Editor	Jeanne Brondino
Editor	Alexandra Mummery
Senior Marketing Associate	Reina Santana
Rights Coordinator	Candace Groskreutz
Customer Service Manager	Christina Sverdrup
Order Fulfillment	Washul Lakdhon
Administrator	Theresa Nelson
Computer Support	Peter Eichelberger
Publisher	Kiran S. Rana

Manufactured in the United States of America

10 9 8 7 6 5   First Edition   13 14 15 16

Contents

List of Illustrations

List of Exercises

DEDICATION

Because they've nurtured me, loved me,
and supported me in all of my efforts,
this book is dedicated to my parents,
Charles G. Fulbright and Ósk Lárusdóttir Fulbright,
and to my grandparents,
Lárus Kristinn Jónsson and Gudmunda Fridsemd Jónasdóttir,
Carl L. Fulbright and Lottie Chapman Fulbright.

Important Note

The material in this book is intended to provide a review of information regarding sexuality. Every effort has been made to provide accurate and dependable information. We believe that the advice given in this book poses no risk to any healthy person. However, if you have any sexually transmitted diseases, we recommend consulting your doctor before using this book.

The publisher, author, and editors, as well as the professionals quoted in the book, cannot be held responsible for any error, omission, professional disagreement, or dated material, and are not liable for any damage, injury, or other adverse outcome of applying any of the information in this book. If you have questions concerning the application of the information described in this book, consult a qualified professional.

Acknowledgments

There are a number of people I would like to thank for making this book possible.

To everyone at Hunter House for believing in me and for helping to cultivate healthy sexuality. In 2003, they took a chance on an aspiring sex expert, and I am forever touched by the time and devotion they've dedicated to my first two books. Special thanks go to publisher Kiran Rana, acquisitions editor Jeanne Brondino, editor Kelley Blewster, editor Alex Mummery, and senior marketing associate Reina Santana for making this second project happen.

To all of my family members for their continued loving support, particularly in the last year—my parents, Charles G. Fulbright and Ósk Lárusdóttir Fulbright, my brother, Xavier Þór Fulbright, my soon-to-be sister-in-law, Lauren Bryson, my grandfather, Carl L. Fulbright, and my relatives in Iceland, Eydís Kristín Sveinbjarnardóttir, Sigurdur Snævarr, Þórunn Sveinbjarnardóttir, Anna Sveinbjarnardóttir, Sveinbjörn Thorarensen, and Sigurlaug "Silla" Thorarensen.

To Bianca Angelino Grimaldi for being my rock.

To Rick Barth, Tiffany J. Franklin, and Andy and Marci Hunn for always being there.

To my nonblood sister, Danielle Cavallucci, for her talent, vision, and infectious smile.

To Solveig Bergh, Casey Chamberlain, Sean Duffy, Melissa Eaton, Cheri Fowler, Frances Harber, Danielle Harms, Jamie Hess, Dara Holtzman, Christy Kiely, Chris Klimek, Dr. Amanda Meulenberg, Vieng Rattanong, Ásgeir Sigfússon, Laura Sutton, and Leana Wen for their love, support, and friendship.

To my yoga and acupressure models Paula D. Atkinson and Gregory Stuart; to illustrators Lisa Kroin and Alexis McQuilkin; and to my father, photographer Charles G. Fulbright, for helping to make this book visually appealing and clear.

To Bryson Coles and Brian Peppler at Snowday Designs for a super website.

To Dr. Steve Chandler for helping me to find my niche in contributing to AASECT, and for hooking me up with lots of books!

Prologue

The popular press always loves a good erotic spot, and they regularly celebrate the "latest" way to drive your lover crazy with just the right touch of a bodily button. Hardly a month goes by without magazine stories announcing a "new" must-test erogenous zone, with results practically guaranteed to rock your world and your sex life. The public responds with bated breath, hoping that maybe this time they will be astounded, their love lives transformed forever. Such articles sell publications because there is a great desire and a great need for better loving, better relationships, and better communication between lovers everywhere.

As a sex expert, I am often asked to provide comments for magazine articles on where to touch one's partner for the best sensations ever and, more importantly, how to do it with the skill and expertise of a sexologist. But whether questions are posed by a journalist, one of my students, a visitor to my Sexuality Source website, or an audience member at one of my speaking engagements, people always want to know: Where should I touch him? Why am I not doing this right? How should I stimulate her? How long till we see results? What other—and better—ways can this be done? Is it possible to be orgasmic—or more orgasmic? That's why I was really excited to tackle a book that brings it all together, a first-of-its-kind work that offers people of all orientations everywhere a one-stop resource exclusively devoted to all of the human body's hottest spots and how to turn them on.

Since I've been writing, lecturing, and working with the media about sex and relationships for over a decade, I put a lot of pressure on myself to keep things stimulating. It can be all too easy to take it for granted that dealing with sex automatically makes my commentary and content sexy —and that people are going to stay tuned in just because it's about sex. So to keep both of us engaged throughout this book and to truly show the rich depth of our sexual nature and erogenous zones, I go way beyond the "what is where" and the "how to turn it on" and delve deeper into the topic of hot spots by fusing together beliefs and practices from different disciplines, primarily tantra, yoga, reflexology, and acupressure. In essence, this book gives people the "CliffsNotes" understanding of sexual intimacy they've longed for while letting them get right to the fun part of turning themselves and their lover(s) on.

Whether you're a novice or seasoned lover, whether you're after self-pleasuring or making all of your lover's wishes come true, this read should prove irresistible. It presents all of the female and male erogenous zones, as well as all of the hot spots shared by the sexes. For each spot, where appropriate, I discuss what makes that particular erogenous zone such a big deal, whether it's related to a specific type of orgasm, the rules for playing with it, and how to effectively stimulate it for the best results, whether it is with your finger, hand, tongue, or another body part that might surprise you. In addition, I am particularly excited about the information I've included on incorporating acupressure and yoga action into your sex play. Although many people are aware that these holistic practices are good for you, many don't realize how amazing they can be for your sex life. In this book, you will learn just how!

Your Hot Spots in Perspective

How to stimulate one's hot spots, whether your own or your lover's, can be a piece of cake—that is, once you know the recipe. The secret to becoming a rave-inspiring "master chef" in the bedroom is knowing when (and how) to throw in a dash of this or a pinch of that, turn up the heat, let things simmer a bit, or even mix up the ingredients. It's also important to know why the right blend makes things so sweet. This book gives you all of the tools you need to make sure that you and your lover are sexually satisfied. It also incorporates information from tantra, yoga, acupressure, and reflexology. Think of these as "secret ingredients" that will help you create your orgasmic masterpiece.

In addition to being a sex educator, I consider myself a lifelong learner. In this book I offer not only facts I've learned while training to be a sexologist, but also lessons I've picked up in my journey to becoming more sexually enlightened myself. In the middle of my doctoral training at NYU, after having answered countless questions through my sex column in the student newspaper and on various sexuality websites, I found myself hungering for something more—for better, richer answers. Cookie-cutter, basic, "you-just-do-this" answers that every other "sexpert" spouts were not enough. I felt that the people I'm serving deserve more. Lovers everywhere want to learn more in their quest to understand themselves as sexual beings, so I decided to write a sex book that would go into greater detail than others and that would cover *all* the body's hot spots, not just the ones people are most familiar with. The result is the volume you hold in your hands.

With so many erogenous zones seriously neglected (besides the genitals and breasts), it is important to learn about all of our erotic spots, from head to toe. With the right amount of time and attention, a plethora of seemingly innocent areas of the body can trigger results ranging from nipple hardening to tingling nerve activation to otherworldly orgasm. By positively embracing the erotic potential of any part of the human body, new lovers can begin their sexual relationship with even more fireworks, and longer-term partners can reactivate the sparks and passion that initially helped bring them together. Whether it's your first or your ten-thousandth time together, with this book you'll embark upon never-imagined, wonder-filled sexual adventures that trump anything you've ever known—as long as we establish an agreement of sorts.

What You Must Promise

As we journey through this book together, I need for you to promise me three things. First, it's important to realize that when it comes to orgasmic hot spots, people tend to limit their erotic potential to the genitals. And although your groin and reproductive organs are full of climactic triggers, you need to conceptualize your body as a vast landscape of Touch-Me-There (or -Here) spots. While taking a tour through every area, every crevice, every inner working, you must see the human body as a vibrant energy source, full of simmering hot spots just waiting for eruptive release. It is only then that you can find all of your and your lover's most titillating erogenous zones. Only then will you discover that the human body is a personal paradise, knowledge that will open you up to a new realm of sexual exploration and experiences.

Furthermore, you need to take your time exploring these wondrous islands. Know that these are the first of many amazing trips to come and that pleasuring a spot or two, not even necessarily a major hot spot, may be as satisfying or even more so than the sex play you're used to. No matter what the spot is, don't *always* approach stimulating it as merely a "pregame" activity, even though it may serve that purpose some of the time. It is important to realize that any of the exercises in this book can be the main event. Intimacy does not need to involve intercourse—or orgasm for that matter—for it to be deemed sex, complete, or "successful." Being able to stay in the moment—attentive to what's present rather than to what's to come or where things might be going—will make your encounter all the more fulfilling.

Second, you must be willing to reevaluate how you communicate in your relationship(s) and how your communication can be improved. People are generally not taught how to communicate effectively in intimate relationships. On the whole, humans are terrible at letting others know how they're truly feeling, what they're really thinking, and what they absolutely need. There's so much threat, so much fear—and things get even more complicated when it comes to a taboo subject like sex! Letting your needs, wants, desires, and turn-offs be known can be one of the most intimidating, difficult things to do, especially if you're worried about bruising the ego of someone you love. Often, sexual communication boils down to a guessing game, full of assumptions. If you want to take charge of your erogenous zones and find your lover's, you must be willing to practice some of the communication strategies offered in this book. It is okay to let your lover know what feels good, to tell your partner how and where to touch you—and how and where *not* to touch you. It's equally okay to let your lover know what doesn't feel good or what isn't working. The trick is in *how* it's communicated, as this book will show.

The need to communicate effectively cannot be emphasized enough, so throughout the book I will provide tips to help you and your lover check in with each other. For now, let me highlight some basic communication techniques:

❄ Never deliver feedback that's critical. Not only are critical comments hurtful, but they are also unlikely to give you the response you're after. Use constructive criticism; for example, "I like the way this feels, and I am thinking that rubbing it more this way will make it feel out of this world."

❄ Use aids in communicating. For example, show your lover specifically what you'd like to do or have done, perhaps based on something you've read in this book. Introducing feedback as an idea instead of as something that needs to be improved upon will keep positive energy flowing.

✳ Remember that nonverbal cues are a form of communication. Moving your lover's hand, applying pressure over your lover's fingers, or breathing more heavily are all ways to let your lover know what you'd like and how you're reacting.

✳ Say "Stop" when you need to, and then say some encouraging words to restart the action. Have an agreement ahead of time that the two of you will check in with each other about whether or not more stimulation is needed.

✳ Listen to each other. Don't get so caught up in your own satisfaction and desires that you're not paying attention to your partner's needs. Tuning out can truly kill the moment.

Now to the third part of our agreement: To get the most out of this book you need to be open-minded. Societal myths and taboos, as well as research findings that make generalizations, often influence people's sexplay exploration, limiting their experiences, pleasure, and orgasmic potential. For many people, erotic areas have more to do with what they've experienced or been told than with what they're open to, further stifling their acceptance of new ideas and possible sensations. So it's important to be open to new information that challenges preconceived notions about what can be a turn-on and what you should or shouldn't do in bed. As we uncover your body's hot spots, we'll demystify some of these myths, allowing you to better decide if certain sex acts are right for you and your partner. We'll also tackle taboos that can prevent lovers from finding novel forms of pleasure.

What You Must Know

The following few pages contain some of the book's most important information. Think of this material as foundational knowledge that will help you perform the exercises in a more meaningful, rewarding way.

This book is rooted in practices for relaxation, healing, and sexual satisfaction that focus on the body's energy centers and erogenous zones. It pulls together concepts utilized in tantric sex, yoga, acupressure, and reflexology. It is hoped that exposure to these overlapping yet diverse perspectives will help you discover and stimulate your and your partner's hot spots even more effectively, with even more tremendous results. Understanding how different parts of the body, including erotic areas, are interconnected and how they influence and stimulate each other helps to frame each hot spot's erogenous qualities and its potential to contribute to better sex and intimacy. Rushing straight to a spot without utilizing the essential knowledge included in this book robs lovers of an opportunity to realize an area's full power to create amazing physical sensations, to deliver an improved and healthier state of mind, and to nurture the spirit. Tapping into this information can give individuals and couples alike a full menu of ways to experience and express their sexuality, feelings, and energy.

Many moons ago, sexual pleasure was used as a tool to build a healthier, more invigorated body and as a way for lovers to become more deeply in tune with themselves and each other. Sexual practices involving exercise and massage were cultivated to strengthen the sexual organs and the body's senses and to support relationships. In this spirit, I've included discussions and activities throughout the book that will serve as a framework not only to help erotic areas feel sensational, but ultimately to generate much more intimacy between you and your partner—physically, emotionally, sexually, and spiritually.

Let's take our first plunge into some of those important concepts.

Tantric Energy Centers

Tantra is an ancient Eastern spiritual practice that seeks to foster sexual energy by merging sex with the spirit. Tantric sex uses the powerful force of intimacy between partners, often released in the form of orgasm, as a fuel for personal transformation and self-realization. In the tantric tradition, the path to stimulating one's energies starts with understanding the body's chakras. The Sanskrit word "chakra," meaning "wheel," "disc," or "hub," describes the seven major and minor centers of psychic energy. They are located along the "shushumna," the fiery central energy meridian, or pathway, that runs up and down the spine (see Figure 1.1). The chakras are affiliated with organs of the endocrine (hormonal) system, since it is these glands that regulate vitality and energy flow. Often depicted as energy vortexes or "whirlpools," chakras vibrate or spin with the energy type that corresponds with their location. They are connected via invisible channels called "nadis."

FIGURE 1.1: The chakras

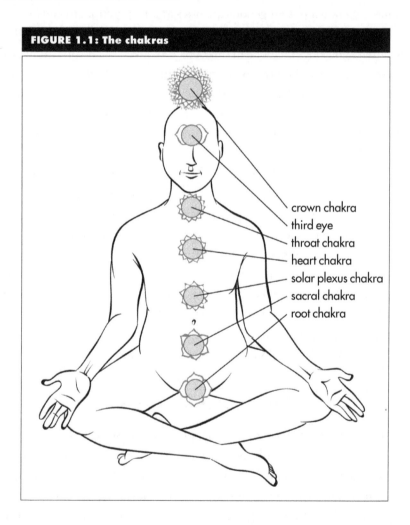

crown chakra
third eye
throat chakra
heart chakra
solar plexus chakra
sacral chakra
root chakra

The Chakras

Chakra 1—Root Chakra (houses all sexual organs and functions in men and some organs and functions in women)
Sanskrit name: *Muladhara*
Location: at the base of the spine (corresponds with sexual center)
Related endocrine gland: ovaries/testes
Energy: basic life and survival energy, including the need to reproduce
Color: red (represents the life force in its powerful, inexplicable form)
Scent: musk

Chakra 2—Sacral Chakra
Sanskrit name: *Swadhisthana*
Location: just above the sexual organs/below the navel
Related endocrine gland: pancreas
Energy: sexual/emotional energy, especially as it relates to a woman's sexual confidence, intuition, and functioning
Color: orange (the color of joy and vitality)
Scent: myrrh (aromatic gum resin of a tree found in Eastern Africa and Arabia)

Chakra 3—Solar Plexus Chakra
Sanskrit name: *Manipura*
Location: between the navel and the base of the sternum
Related endocrine gland: adrenals
Energy: personal power and how we use it; is connected to one's ego
Color: yellow (cheerfulness and radiance)
Scent: amber

Chakra 4—Heart Chakra
Sanskrit name: *Anahata*
Location: the heart
Related endocrine gland: thymus
Energy: female in aspect, related to how we give and receive love and affection; regulates breathing and circulation
Color: green and rose (hope, rebirth, and creativity)
Scent: rose

Chakra 5—Throat Chakra

Sanskrit name: *Vishuddha*

Location: the throat

Related endocrine gland: thyroid/parathyroid

Energy: masculine in aspect, related to creativity and expression; the chakra of living and speaking your truth; controls one's voice and ability to communicate

Color: turquoise or Russian blue

Scent: frankincense (fragrant gum resin of a tree found in Somalia and southern coastal Arabia)

Chakra 6—Third Eye

Sanskrit name: *Ajna*

Location: the "third-eye" (middle) region of the forehead

Related endocrine gland: pituitary

Energy: inner light/spiritual intuition; related to physical and psychic vision

Color: deep blue

Scent: jasmine

Chakra 7—Crown Chakra

Sanskrit name: *Sahasrara*

Location: the crown of the head

Related endocrine gland: pineal

Energy: connection to spiritual truth, existence, pure consciousness, and emotional and mental enlightenment

Color: violet or pure white

Scent: lotus

The chakras, representing the dynamic flow of cosmic energy within the body, are a must-know component of stimulating your hot spots. When the chakras are healthy, one's sexual relations are vibrant. The chakras contribute to one's sexual aura, which, in turn, becomes sexual chemistry between two people. When opening, stimulating, and balancing the chakras, you can feel your own and your lover's aura, presence, and sexual vitality.

As a warm-up for the activities in this book, try the following two exercises, which are designed to help you get a better sense of the energy and chakras you'll be working with.

⟐ EXERCISE 1.1: *Finding Your Energy*

Practice the following exercise, first by yourself, and then, if appropriate, with your partner. Be sure to take your time and to do the exercise in a quiet space that is free from distractions.

1. Sit in a comfortable position, and hold your hands up in the prayer position, but with palms only facing each other, not touching.

2. Breathe in deeply and steadily.

3. Send your breath out toward your hands, imagining this exhalation as heat, a vibration, or light.

4. Notice the magnetic charge that is building between your palms.

5. Close your eyes and relish this charge for a few moments.

6. Repeat with your partner. As you face each other, create energy between your hands and those of your lover.

⟐ EXERCISE 1.2: *Sensing Your Lover's Aura*

1. With your eyes open, sit beside your lover and move your hands slowly around their body without actually touching it.

2. Keeping your palms open and relaxed, approximately an inch or two above the skin, sense the aura coming off your beloved's body—the heat, light, density, tingling. You may even experience it as visual imagery or color.

3. Notice the difference in physical sensations as you move nearer to one of the chakras.

4. Repeat, but this time with your eyes closed.

5. Have your partner do the same to you.

6. Repeat steps 1–5, this time focusing on the seven chakras. Can you feel the energy emanating out of these areas? Can you visualize it?

7. As you hover over each center, ask your partner to concentrate on

the area and to visualize its color (see the chakra descriptions above). What is going on there? What kind of energy is being exuded?

Yoga

Throughout this book, where appropriate, I suggest yoga poses for couples, some of which are related to advanced sexual positions utilized in tantric sexual practice. Yoga can enliven your sexual desire, ignite or reignite your love and passion, and heighten your pleasure and level of intimacy. While some couples may want to try these exercises just for kicks, others may see them as a way to redefine what is sexual; as a new way to experience each other's body, with or without clothes; and as a new way to bond. When done properly, yoga poses also improve flexibility and sexual ability; performed regularly, postures that exercise the hips, thighs, and groin make it easier to engage in certain lovemaking positions. Plus, exercise in and of itself is often considered an aphrodisiac.

Although engaging with your partner in yoga poses can turn you on, keep in mind that the greater goal is to connect. This is possible because these positions help lovers to open their heart, sacral, and root chakras, releasing dormant sexual energy and increasing their capacity to embrace and love their partner. The more familiar you are with the chakras, your body's energy, and how to channel that energy with your breath, the more you'll get out of doing the yoga positions and the more you'll utilize your sexual energy during sex play. Yoga's emphasis on breathing, movement, and spiritual communion increases the flow of *prana* (life energy) throughout your body. Hence, it also helps to cleanse and tone the sexual organs, keeping lovers healthy and sexually vigorous.

Yoga provides a different way of becoming intimate, of getting to know your partner's body. As lovers move through the recommended positions, becoming pressed together at times, they are able to see each other in a whole new light. At the same time, yoga helps your body unwind and feel good, possibly heightening your desire to make love. This interaction also helps to expand the idea of what sex is about, making it a full-body experience instead of merely a genitalia-focused one.

Acupressure

Centuries ago, Chinese doctors observed that muscular tension typically accumulated around specific points, blocking the body's energy from circulating freely. Acupressure was developed to eliminate toxins held in muscle tissue, thereby increasing blood flow and energy. Special techniques for holding and touching major body points help to relieve pain and promote healing, relaxation, and increased sexual energy. Acupressure can be used by lovers to intensify pleasurable physical sensations and transform sexual energy, leading to greater healing and intimacy and deepening bonds of trust and compassion.

According to the principles of traditional Chinese medicine, health is maintained by the smooth, unimpeded flow of life energy throughout the body's meridians; acupressure uses "acupoints," which can be thought of as doorways into and out of the body, to correct or restore this flow when necessary. Acupoints are the entry points into what are known as "meridians," channels that keep the body's skin, muscles, and organs—as well as the psyche—healthy and in balance by transporting this life energy, known as *qi, ki,* or *chi.* In conjunction with the flow of blood and bodily fluids, chi nourishes the whole system. Acupressure involves the firm but gentle stimulation of acupoints with the practitioner's fingers, thumbs, elbows, or feet. After an acupressure session, the restored flow of chi is sometimes experienced as a warm, tingly, heavy sensation followed by relaxation. (Acupuncture, the practice of inserting fine needles into the skin to promote healing, utilizes the body's same acupoints.)

Acupressure can be used by couples to improve their sexual chemistry and the quality of their relationship. Using your finger or hand, apply slow, gradual pressure to your lover's pressure points. (Note: Do not pull the skin or use fingers with long nails.) Both partners should take long, slow, deep breaths in unison. Maintain the pressure on an acupoint for one to five minutes, gradually applying more of your body weight. This causes the system to release endorphins, neurochemicals that are the body's natural painkillers, creating a euphoric high. It also allows oxygen and other nutrients to better nourish the body, naturally heightening one's eroticism and sexual responsiveness, connectedness, and vitality. It is the clear flow of energy through the body's meridians that results in more radiance, sensuality, and intimacy.

An acupressure point can feel sore when pressure is applied. Be sure to ask your partner to let you know if they experience any tenderness. If your partner would like for you to continue, do so with slow, careful pressure so that a spot doesn't become too sore.

To locate the acupoints, keep in mind that most will be along a bone indentation or protrusion. Don't press directly on a bone unless you feel an indentation in the hollow of the bone. Other points are mostly located underneath major muscle groups, which can be found by feeling for a muscular cord or slight indentation between tendon and muscle. Once an acupoint is found, press it slowly and directly.

Reflexology

The components of one's total self—the body, mind, and spirit—are nourished and replenished by sexual energy. Whether regarded as life force, breath, air, energy, or vital essence, chi is the life-giving force that creates movement and maintains the universe. Working with this energy is what contributes to one's overall state of happiness. Sexual reflexology cultivates the expression of energy that will better one's mind, body, and spirit. It works with the body's sexual energy and the way it manifests itself in the body, and its role in health and well-being has been recognized by Taoists for the last five thousand years.

The general premise of reflexology is that all of the body's organs have reflex points located on other body parts. Organs in one area of the body can be stimulated by working the reflexes in a corresponding reflex-point area. Sexual reflex points, the most powerful and strongest of which are the sexual organs, draw upon the body's best energy since the entire body is involved in feeding the sexual center with energy. When stimulated, the sexual reflex points have a powerful healing effect on one's organs and senses. Sex acts, such as intercourse, become a form of "ecstatic" acupressure, in that the entire body pumps the sexual organs full of energy when they are stimulated, promoting general relaxation and releasing endorphins, which help the body to feel good. Taoists see sexual intimacy as a healing practice, the cultivation of sexual energy for the body, mind, and spirit that ultimately leads to a healthier, sexier individual.

There are four basic techniques used in reflexology, two of which you can use on many of the hot spots described in this book. (Most of us are familiar with reflexology that is performed on the feet and hands, but you can think of the whole body as your playing field.) As with any other exercise, you'll get better with practice, so don't be afraid to practice on yourself!

1. Thumb walking—Bend the first joint of your thumb (the one closest to the tip), being careful not to bend the second joint (the one at the base). Holding the thumb below the first joint will help. Bend and unbend it a few times in midair for practice. Place the outside edge of your thumb on the skin of the area you wish to stimulate, rocking it from the tip of the thumb to the lower edge of the nail. "Walk" the thumb forward by bending and unbending the first joint, being careful not to push the thumb. You want it to inch along, using firm pressure. Check in with your partner to see if the pressure needs to be adjusted; what feels good will change depending on the body part being stimulated and the person's sensitivity.

2. Finger walking—Bend your index finger at the first joint (the one closest to the tip) only. Holding the finger below the first knuckle may help. Bend and unbend in midair for practice. Then place the tip of your finger on the part of the body you wish to stimulate, and rock from the fingertip to the lower edge of the fingernail. "Walk" the finger forward by bending and unbending the first joint without pushing the finger. Check in with your partner to see if more or less pressure is desired. Also, avoid digging into the skin with your fingernail.

Hot-Spot Send-Off

The full scope of tantra, yoga, acupressure, and reflexology goes far beyond what is presented in this book. Yet key components of each are brought together here in an attempt to interweave the many facets of mind, body, and spirit that make an erogenous zone so incredibly hot. I have drawn upon these disciplines in the hope that you will become better able to stimulate your body and your lover's body, expand your sexual energy, and have a more blissful, gratifying sensual experience overall.

With all of this in mind, we're ready for a guided tour of the body's wild attractions and eruptive reactions. Chapters 2 through 4 take you through all of *her* orgasmic hot spots, namely the clitoris, G-spot, A-spot, urethra, cervix, and labia. Chapters 5 through 7 focus on *his* orgasmic spots, primarily the frenulum, corona, foreskin, prostate, perineum, and testicles. Chapters 8 through 12 celebrate mind-blowing spots on both sexes, covering the breasts, head, torso, anus, hands, and feet. This part of the book will titillate your imagination about new possibilities for warming up to great sex or for making the hot spots the main event. So, again, don't take the order of the chapters as an indication of the sequence in which you should approach their content. Feel free to fool around! Chapters 13 and 14 wrap things up by describing sex toys and sexual positions. Lastly, the Resources and Recommended Reading section, located at the back of the book, provides a list of sources for more information on many of the topics discussed in this book. It also lists retail outlets where you can buy the products mentioned in the text.

All of the following chapters aim to

* show you how to find Mother Nature's often-hidden treasures and maximize their pleasure
* offer a plethora of sex facts and tips
* provide you with techniques and fresh ideas about how to use and/or stimulate each area effectively
* enable you to become a better communicator and lover
* release you from any notions of what you "can't" do
* help you build intimacy with both yourself and your lover

As we visit each of the body's hot spots, we'll cover a variety of sexual behaviors, dive into a wide range of ways to enhance sex, explore different types of fantasy, and practice exercises that will help you to become more orgasmic and sexually satisfied. As you read through each chapter, engaging in the exercises of your choosing, take a moment to reconceptualize what it means to be intimate, what total-body intimacy can offer you and your partner. This is one guided tour you won't want to miss!

Her Must-Know, Volcanic Hot Spot

The **clitoris** (C-spot) is a highly sensitive sexual organ. Even though the visible part is only ¾ to 1¼ inches long, it is filled with nearly eight thousand nerve endings. This crown jewel sits right in front of the vaginal entrance and urethra, just beneath the point where the inner lips meet, and it extends into the body. It consists of (1) the **clitoral glans** (or **glans clitoris**), the visible, external tip or crown, which is the most sensitive part of a woman's genitals, and (2) the **clitoral shaft** or **corpus** (body), which contains spongy erectile tissue, specifically a pair of corpora cavernosa (the same tissue that is found in the male's penis). The clitoral body extends several centimeters into the internal anatomy, stretching upward and toward the back, before splitting, like a Y, into two longer, thinner parts, known as the **crura**, or "legs." The clitoris's erectile tissue wraps around the vaginal opening, urethra, urethral sponge, and vagina, making the vast majority of the clitoris's five or so inches invisible. Far beyond a simple magic button, the clitoris is meant to electrify a woman's entire reproductive system, if not her entire being, when stimulated.

The clitoris is enveloped by a sheath of tissue, an extension of the inner vulval lips, known as the **clitoral hood**, or **prepuce**. Gently pushing up the clitoral hood provides a better view of the glans. This hood protects the glans, especially from overstimulation. The glans folds into the hood just prior to orgasm, a reaction caused when a suspensory ligament that is attached to both glans and ovaries becomes stretched at peak arousal as the woman's internal reproductive system braces for climax.

The size and appearance of the clitoris varies considerably from woman to woman. It may be as small as a seed pearl or as big as a child's fingertip; some females have what is considered an "enlarged" clitoris. Some protrude more, while others remain more hidden. Some may swell more than the clitoral hood and lips during sexual excitement, becoming more visible and firmer, with the shaft elongating. Others may appear to retreat as the vaginal lips and hood swell to a greater extent. Generally, this pleasure dome becomes more prominent during early sexual arousal and stimulation and then withdraws as a female becomes even more turned on.

Why Is the Clitoris One of the Hottest Spots?

When a woman is sexually aroused, her clitoris swells as it fills with blood; it becomes "erect," doubling in size as it hardens. This is possible because its internal structure consists of spongy, erectile bodies (the paired corpora cavernosa, plus paired clitoral, or vestibular, bulbs beneath the skin of the labia minora at the vaginal opening) that fill with blood. The clitoris is deemed one of the prized hot spots of the female anatomy both because up to 75 percent of women need direct clitoral stimulation in order to climax during intercourse and also because this piece of heaven is so exquisitely sensitive to touch, pressure, and temperature. With its base extending from the top of the pubic bone to the anus, and consisting of extensive supporting tissue that connects it to the mons pubis and labia, the clitoris interacts with some fifteen thousand nerve fibers in a woman's pelvic area. Furthermore, recent research conducted by Australian urologist Dr. Helen O'Connell has confirmed that the vagina is an extension of the clitoris. If skin is lifted off the sidewalls of the vagina, one sees the bulbs of the clitoris—masses of erectile tissue.

Although the clitoris is often regarded as the female's equivalent of the male penis, this notion is not wholly correct and is, in fact, sexist. Unlike the penis, the clitoris has no reproductive or urinary function, and it does not lengthen nearly in the same way as a penis, despite becoming engorged with blood when stimulated. The clitoris and penis do, however, stem from the same embryological tissues. So if we're going to equate body parts, perhaps we should say that the penis is the equivalent of the female's clitoris, non?

Clitoral Orgasm

The **clitoral orgasm**, characterized by involuntary rhythmic contractions of the pubococcygeus muscle (PC muscle), is wildly popular. This is because about 90 percent of women can have an orgasm from direct clitoral stimulation. Also known as the **vulvic** or **vulval orgasm**, it is considered the most reliable, easily obtainable, and most insatiable of the female orgasms, especially since it often produces multiple orgasms. This is because the clitoral orgasm is triggered by the body's pudendal nerve and because the clitoris is centrally attached to the urethra and vagina. These three areas together form a tissue cluster that researchers believe is central to female sexual function and orgasm. It is also believed that the repeated stimulation of the glans clitoris evokes a uterine reflex response, known as the clitorouterine reflex, which is yet another component of a woman's sexual response. Thus, it is no wonder that clitoral orgasms create the most sensation in the lower one-third of a woman's vagina.

The practice of reflexology sees the clitoris as corresponding to the kidneys and bladder. Stimulating the clitoral area excessively is said to tax the kidneys, possibly causing water retention, bladder infection, or weight problems.

Clitoral Myths and Misconceptions

Myth: Masturbation causes the clitoris to enlarge.
Although the clitoris may temporarily become larger when stimulated, masturbation does not cause permanent clitoral enlargement.

Myth: A larger clitoris makes for more intense sexual arousal.
A clitoris is highly erogenous no matter what its size.

Myth: Only neurotic women have clitoral orgasms.
Psychoanalyst Sigmund Freud was wrong when he said clitoral stimulation is for adolescent girls and that only mature women learn to transfer erotic sensations to the vagina. Every woman, of every age and maturity level, has the potential to enjoy clitoral orgasm.

Myth: All women respond to clitoral stimulation.
While the overwhelming majority of women enjoy clitoral stimulation and orgasm, not every woman will find it a hot spot, and a woman should not be made to feel less of a woman or less sexual if this is true for her.

Myth: Clitoral piercings make for more orgasmic sex.
If you're considering getting a clitoral hood piercing, know that research has found *no* dramatic difference in orgasmic functioning in women who have one. There is a positive relationship, however, between a vertical clitoral-hood piercing and the woman's sexual desire, frequency of intercourse, and arousal.

Clitoral Stimulation

Playing with the clitoris is often the key to any satisfying sexual romp. If it is bypassed during foreplay, the chances of a woman attaining climax are not nearly as great. Before going right for the clitoris, however, it's important to know a couple of things. First, make sure you know the rules of clitoral play (see below). And second, seduce the clitoris. A lover should never just home in on the clit and go to town. Like a good meal, the main course is always a little tastier when you're hungry for it. While clitoral play is often a form of foreplay, a woman's whole anatomy usually needs a little warm-up before the clitoris is able to offer its treasures. Working the entire vulval area before concentrating on any part, especially the clitoris, makes for a much better, body-tingling sexual experience—and response!

Whether it's your own vulva or somebody else's, start by placing your hand over the genitals, your fingers pointed toward the woman's backside. Massage the entire area, pulling your hand up toward the belly, then pressing on the mons pubis as you push back down. This motion provides indirect sensations to the clitoris. Start out slowly and gently, steadily getting faster and faster and applying more and more pressure. A woman will enjoy the heat produced by this action. After a while, let your fingers start to wander. Apply pressure with your fingertips to each area as you explore, saving the clitoris for last. Then, lightly tickle the clitoris, pressing your fingers intermittently on the surrounding areas, before you work your magic with your fingers or tongue while performing the exercises that appear on the following pages.

Rules for Clitoral Play

✳ Take care that your nails have been trimmed, leaving no hangnails or rough edges.

✳ Make sure you're stimulating the right part (not the urethral opening).

✳ Although steady rhythm is effective, don't rub this hot spot like you're trying to remove a stain. Experiment with different types of fondling, realizing that different touches may feel good at different times and from one sexual experience to the next.

✳ Make sure you use plenty of lubricant. The vagina often doesn't produce enough natural lubrication, especially around the clitoral area. Working a dry clitoris, especially over a long period of time, can make it feel raw, irritated, and even sore. Having a tube of water-based Astroglide or silicone-based Eros handy, or even using your own spit, will help to keep things smooth and comfortable. Baby oil or petroleum jelly are also options, but be aware that the oil in these products can cause both latex condoms and dental dams to deteriorate.

✳ Be careful not to apply too much direct pressure to the clitoris, since this can cause pain or irritation in some states of arousal. You may need to ease off every now and then. Sometimes indirect stimulation is much more pleasurable, so try rubbing the sides of the clitoris and the inner lips instead.

✳ Communicate with your partner! Every woman is different. What may have worked for one may not work for another, and only your lover can tell you what feels good or painful. This will be especially important as she experiences more intense sensations and moves closer to the Big O, a time when direct pressure on the clitoris may become too much.

✽ Communicate with yourself! Get to know your clitoris. Make sure you're familiar with what turns you on and what kinds of pressure, stimulation, and sensations your clitoris likes, so you can share the info with your lover. Also, be sure to make a date with your clitoris on more than one occasion. What you find you enjoy when you're tired may be totally different from what strikes a special chord when you're already sexually charged, so it's good to know what your body likes under different circumstances. Having this knowledge makes it easier for you to teach your lover about your body and your needs.

✽ If it's your clitoris, don't get too caught up in yourself at the expense of missing out on your lover's reactions to turning you on. Many partners find clitoral play highly arousing, sometimes so much so that it brings them to the point of orgasm themselves! So enjoy watching your adored one smiling, glowing, concentrating on, and basking in—simply spellbound by—the joys of clitoral wonder.

Give a little demonstration of what feels good. As you do so, ask your partner to cup their hand over yours in order to feel your rhythm, energy, and motions. As you eventually allow your lover to take over, don't be afraid to guide the hand motion, all the while offering affirmative or constructive feedback, saying, for example, "I like your rhythm, but now I need just a little more pressure."

Finger Action for Clitoral Pleasure

◀ EXERCISE 2.1: *Ride 'Em Cowgirl*

1. Place your hand between her legs and cup her buttocks in your palm, resting your wrist and lower forearm against her vulva.

2. Ask her if she wants to "ride" your wrist or the heel of your hand, pressing herself against you. This allows her to control the pressure against her vulva and clitoris.

3. Soon after you've picked up on her rhythm, offer to take over, pressing your arm against her vulva as you massage other hot spots. If she wants to continue getting herself off, by all means, don't interrupt!

As an alternative, instead of using your arm, slip your leg between her legs so that she can ride your thigh or knee.

❦ EXERCISE 2.2: *Playing Her Like a Twelve-String Guitar*

1. Use the thumb and index finger of one hand to part her labia while moving your other hand's index and/or middle finger in a gentle circling motion around her clitoris. You'll notice that, with increased arousal, her clitoris will become firmer. Her verbal and nonverbal reactions will determine how much pressure you should use and how soon you may want to move on to step 2. If she enjoys this motion, stay with it for a while. If it becomes too much, move on to the next step. If it's unclear what she's experiencing, ask her.

2. Rub the clitoral shaft, moving up and down between the hood and base, keeping your movement firm and steady.

3. Intermittently, rock your fingertip back and forth across the glans, applying pressure directly on it or from the side (closer to the root), as though massaging your temples.

4. At any point, unless her clitoris is feeling super-sensitive, tap against the clitoris rhythmically with your finger(s) or hand. Depending on her preferred style of stimulation, she may enjoy a steady smacking or slapping action against her clitoris, but this action may be more bearable—yet still quite effective—if she has clothes on. You may also get more of a reaction if her mons pubis bears part of this love tap, as doing so will remove some of the force from her clitoris.

The clitoral hood can be regarded as its own hot spot since it, too, fills with blood during sexual arousal, as demonstrated in the following exercise.

◀ EXERCISE 2.3: *What's under Here? Getting to Know the Clitoral Hood*

1. Rub the clitoris and clitoral hood gently between your thumb and index finger. Play around with it like one of those tiny scraps of paper you find yourself mindlessly rolling into a ball on occasion. However, be mindful of the finger action. Ask her if she'd like more or less pressure.

2. Give the clit a break every now and then by pulling the clitoral hood back and forth with your thumb and index finger. The friction created by this type of stimulation will be powerful, and you may find her catching her breath. Head nods from her are perfectly acceptable at this point when trying to gauge what feels good to her.

3. Carry on by holding and squeezing the clitoris between the thumb and index finger of one hand. Use the middle and ring fingers of either hand in a rubbing motion along the clitoral shaft. Note: Her clitoris may not be long enough for this move, and that's okay.

Other moves you can use during clitoral stimulation may include arching your thumb backward to stimulate the clitoris while inserting your middle and ring fingers into her vagina. If you're able to rhythmically provide pressure to the inner front wall of her vagina at the same time, you may trigger a reaction from her G-spot (which we'll discuss in the next chapter). Longer hands may be able to simultaneously stimulate the rectal area in place of the vagina. When doing this, move the middle and ring fingers the same way you moved them in the vagina.

Always thoroughly wash the fingers and hands that you've used to stimulate the anal area before inserting (or reinserting) them into the vagina. Failing to do so may transmit bacteria that can cause infection.

You can also try placing the heel of your hand on her mons pubis, exerting pressure as you move it back and forth during clitoral stimulation. This will create different sensations, especially in the clitoral hood's movements. Also, stroking, rubbing, or tugging at her inner and outer vaginal lips will produce a variety of feel-good reactions.

A woman does not experience a refractory period after orgasm, during which she is unable to become aroused again. Rather, she can experience her full sexual-response cycle again and again, making it possible for her to climax more than once. So don't be afraid to stimulate the clitoris as much as she can handle it throughout the course of your sexual encounter.

◖ TIPS FOR FINGER PLAY ◗

"Hero worship" warning.
Although the clitoris can produce amazing results, don't worship it. Becoming too consumed with only this spot can cost you points in other lovemaking areas. A woman likes to feel sexy all over, worshipped for the sensuality of her total body and not just reduced to a single spot. So make sure you take the time to show off the breadth of your stimulation skills by paying attention to other parts of her body as well.

Ask away.
In learning about your partner's clitoris, don't be afraid to ask questions. Hopefully she'll welcome the opportunity to let you know how her body is responding and what does and doesn't seem to move heaven and earth for her. So as you stimulate her, go ahead and ask her things like: "Do you want more pressure?" "Is this too intense?" "Am I hurting you?" Have her help you out by telling you what feels incredible for her at that moment and throughout sex play. Encourage her to show you. Reassure her that she can tell you when it's too much as well—you won't be insulted. It's important to stay in tune with each other, since what can be highly satisfying for her one minute can be excruciating the next. What is too fast early on may be too slow as she approaches orgasm. And what may satiate her on one occasion may get a "thumbs down" the next. The clitoris can be, mmmm, shall we say, a bit temperamental at times.

Oral Action for Clitoral Pleasure

One of the best ways to attend to this goddess spot is to perform cunnilingus—oral sex on a woman. There are a number of positions a couple can utilize to provide oodles of orgasm-inducing oral action. The most common is for a woman to lie on her back, legs spread apart and knees bent, with her partner on their knees, bent over and down. Putting one or two pillows under her buttocks, shoulders, or neck, or holding her legs up toward her head can help to make the vulva more easily accessible to you. Such tactics also help to prevent her body from arching as she becomes more aroused, which could change the angle of stimulation, making it less effective and more uncomfortable for the performer. Another position involves the partners lying one on top of the other, facing opposite ways, with the active partner's head curved inward to provide lip-on-lip action, though this can be much more limiting.

Sexual Health Considerations

Several sexually transmitted infections (STIs) can be spread during oral sex, primarily herpes, genital warts, chlamydia, syphilis, gonorrhea, and HIV. Oral sex is considered a high-risk sexual behavior for HIV transmission, especially if a woman is menstruating. There are several things you can do to protect yourself from infection when going down on her:

⊙ *Don't brush or floss your teeth for at least two hours before performing oral sex on somebody. Such oral-hygiene activities can cause cuts or sores in the mouth, raising the risk of contracting an STI. Use a mild mouthwash if you're worried about being kissable.*

⊙ *Consider using a dental dam, e.g., Glyde, Lixx, or Good Vibrations brands. The barrier can be held in place over her vulva with your hands while you go to town. The Dondam is a dental dam that you can stick to your face, allowing you to perform hands-free!*

Trying a new position is always good for novelty's sake and for spicing things up. Here are some other possible positions for cunnilingus:

✲ The woman can stand while her partner crouches down to pleasure her.

✲ She can be propped up on pillows with her partner lying flat on their own stomach, arms propped on a pillow as well.

✲ She can lie down, left leg bent, with her partner sticking their head under the back of her left knee to reach the vulva. Coming at the clitoris from a side angle can also be done with her knees bent, legs pulled up.

✳ The woman can lie on her back as her partner grabs her pelvis or buttocks and pulls up. A variation of this involves draping her legs over her partner's shoulders.

✳ She can straddle her lover's face. Facing her partner's feet allows her to stimulate her lover's genitals with her hands or mouth. (Note: This position becomes the famous *"69"* or *"soixante-neuf"* when she performs oral sex as well!)

As with manual stimulation, you want to hold off on going for the gold right away. Ease into action by kissing and massaging her inner thighs and groin. Kiss and lick her entire genital area, allowing yourself to salivate copiously, before finally moving to the clitoris. As you work your way to her "love button," pant deeply, allowing your warm breath to rhythmically beat against her vulva. The heat will have a yummy effect, with the sensations and the sound of your aroused-beyond-belief breathing turning her on even more. She'll love knowing that you're so into her —and her genitals!

Once you've enjoyed all of this, go nuts with the following exercise. Feel free to take it in stages or to do all of it in one session. There's no rush. With any success, there will surely be encore performances. So make it your number-one goal to please her, and then relish the reactions. You may find that steps 1 and 2 are all it takes for her to climax and be sexually satisfied. Still, be sure to mix things up from time to time by trying out all the steps and tips. Versatility is a must in clitoral play, and a suave lover is able to adapt to a woman's needs instead of simply sticking with the same move on every occasion, even if it's tried-and-true.

❧ EXERCISE 2.4: *Ultimate Lip Service*

1. Gently part her vaginal lips and brush your lips and tongue against her clitoris, tenderly starting to lick the area.

2. Press your lips firmly around her clitoris and gently suck, allowing her to get used to the warmth and wetness. Use your tongue to caress the clitoris.

3. Slowly start to lap at the clit, keeping your tongue soft as you caress it. Moving faster and faster, yet always maintaining a steady rhythm as you intensify the pressure, tighten your tongue as you widen your strokes. Alternate between moving your tongue side to side and up and down.

4. For variety, try stiffening your tongue into a point and darting it at the clitoris as if it were a bull's-eye. Bang the tongue against the clitoris in a thrusting motion as your partner gets more and more excited.

5. If you feel like being a tease, every now and then go back to sucking gently on the clitoris before returning to more rapid action.

6. Insert a lubed finger or two into the vagina or anus for added stimulation.

7. To make things even more intense, stimulate other parts of her body with your hands or sex toys as you're getting her off with your tongue.

Every time you perform this exercise, try different tongue strokes; for example, diagonally across the clitoral head, licking at it like a cat carefully cleaning its paw, or puckering your lips for a suction effect. Adding other sensations to your oral sex feast, depending on the climate in the bedroom, will certainly win you brownie points. On a hot day she may welcome your sucking on a lozenge or an ice cube before going down on her, as it will create a cool, tingly, refreshing sensation. A cold evening may call for warming your tongue with a hot toddy or ginger tea before pressing it against her clit. If it's a can't-get-enough-of-you romp, get noisy and let her know how much you love going down on her. If it's a more mellow encounter, try humming to provide additional stimulation.

❦ TIPS FOR ORAL PLAY ❧

If you have whiskers, shave.

Before stimulating her orally, consider being clean-shaven. Unless you have a soft beard or she likes the coarseness of your facial hair against her genitals and inner thighs, know that stubble can end up irritating the sensitive skin between her legs. She could end up with an uncomfortable "beard burn."

Kiss it. French kiss it!

According to tantric practice, stimulating the clitoris sends sensations to the upper lip of the mouth. So "make out" with her clit as if you were kissing her mouth.

Get into it!

Get your whole face in there. Bury yourself and breathe her in. Work up a sweat. Gorge on her as though she's the best meal you've ever had. She'll be absolutely delighted and will feel more sexually confident knowing that you lust after her.

Stimulate her G-spot at the same time.

As you lavish her clitoris with oral admiration, use a free finger to feel around the inside front wall of her vaginal canal for her G-spot, a.k.a. clitoral cluster. (See Chapter 3 for detailed instructions on locating the G-spot.) As soon as you feel the raised, rough, and swollen area of the G-spot, firmly press your finger(s) against it, providing constant pressure in an up-down or circular motion—all the while becoming even more frenzied with your tongue action.

Pay attention to the details.

The vulva has a couple of parts related to the clitoris that often go unmentioned and are worth taking the time to identify and stimulate. The *front commissure* is the smooth area right above the clitoral hood and head that contains nerve fibers. Another sensitive area that could use some lovin' on occasion is her *clitoral frenulum*, the area right below her clitoral head where the lower division of the inner lips meet. Applying firm pressure and/or massaging these areas with your fingertips and tongue will work wonders.

Use the inside of your upper lip to provide stimulation.

Turning it upward, rest the inner part of your lip against the clitoris, applying more pressure by using the weight of your head, and shake your head back and forth, as if shaking wet hair (or maybe it is wet with sweat!).

Take a breather.

Coming up for air every now and then will help her to feel even more connected to you and will allow you to stimulate other hot spots, like her navel and nipples. It also allows you to see her radiant face—that is, unless you picked the moment just before climax to come up for air....

Acupressure Points

◀ EXERCISE 2.5: *Touch Her There*

Stimulation of the backside's Womb and Vitals acupressure points (see Figure 2.1) benefits a woman's reproductive system, increasing circulation and sexual pleasure throughout her pelvis, and it also nurtures her womb and other reproductive organs. These two points are located one to two finger-widths midway between the top of the buttocks and the top of the hip bone, level with the top of the sacrum.

One of the best ways to stimulate these points while focusing on the clitoris is to have her lie on top of you, facing your feet, as you orally stimulate her. You can also scoop your hands under her buttocks to activate these points if she prefers to be on her back during cunnilingus. In whatever position is most comfortable for the both of you, try holding these points as you slowly make large and small circles with your tongue around her clitoris. As she reaches climax, gently suck on her clit and apply slightly more pressure to these points.

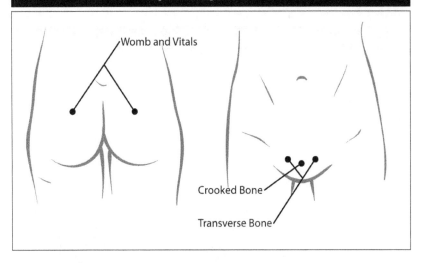

FIGURE 2.1: The locations of the Womb and Vitals, Crooked Bone, and Transverse Bone acupressure points

Womb and Vitals

Crooked Bone

Transverse Bone

◀ EXERCISE 2.6: *Touch Her Here*

There are three other acupressure points on her abdominal side that you can stimulate while performing oral sex (note: these are *not* to be stimulated during pregnancy): the Crooked Bone point, in the center of the top edge of the pubic bone, and the two Transverse Bone points, each half a finger-width from the midline on either side, on the upper border of the pubic bone (see Figure 2.1 on the previous page). Place your fingers on these points as you kneel between your lover's knees. Using your fingers to draw skin away from the pubic bone toward the navel better exposes the clitoris as you begin oral stimulation, kissing, licking, or sucking on the clitoris. Such moves will increase sexual energy and awareness and regulate her reproductive system.

Yoga Poses for Clitoral Stimulation

◀ POSE 2.1: *Clitoral Stimulation and Vaginal Relaxation*

Her position: She is in the Goddess Pose (Supta Baddha Konasana), lying on her back with the soles of her feet together, knees falling out to the sides. She can rest her hands on her belly or on her partner's buttocks.

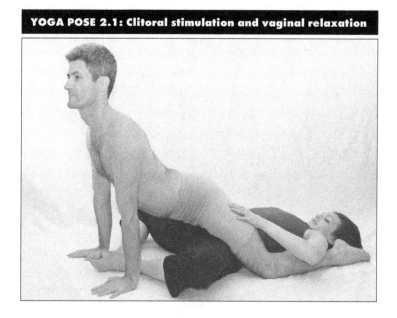

YOGA POSE 2.1: Clitoral stimulation and vaginal relaxation

Her partner's position: Facing the same direction as the bottom partner's feet, her partner is above her in Upward Dog (Urdhva Muhka Svanasana), legs spread along her sides. To get into this position, place your
hands by the bottom partner's feet and lift your upper body so that your
belly or pelvis grazes the area between her legs as you slowly lower your
hips to the ground. Upward Dog involves having your weight distributed
on your lower legs, knees, and hands, with your arms straight and your
back curving upward. Both lovers should breathe deeply, attempting to
synchronize the breath as each inhale and exhale becomes longer, deeper,
and slower. Hold this pose for up to five minutes.

Results: Her vaginal-wall muscles become relaxed and her sexual pleasure
is enhanced, especially as her clitoris is grazed by her lover's lower torso.
Resting her hands on her lower belly will help her to focus her attention
on the sacral chakra, opening and stimulating it, especially as she channels her breath.

◀ POSE 2.2: *Clitoral Stimulation and Heart Connection*

Her partner's position: The lover is in Fish Pose (Matsyasana). Lie on
your back, with your legs straight, toes pointed upward. Lift your pelvis
off the floor enough to slide your hands, palms down, under your buttocks. Tucking your forearms and elbows close to the sides of your torso,
press them against the floor. As you inhale, lift your upper torso and head
away from the floor. Gently place your head back onto the floor so that
the crown rests against it; your back, including the neck, is arched.

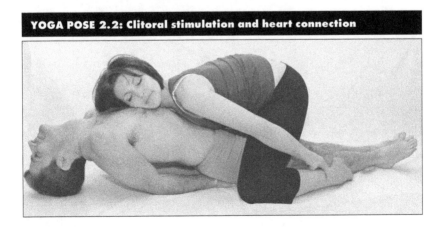

YOGA POSE 2.2: Clitoral stimulation and heart connection

Her position: She straddles her partner's hips, with her heels against her partner's upper thighs in a supported Hero's Pose (Virasana). Inhale and extend your upper body forward over your partner's heart, and lie down on your lover. Your hands are at your sides.

Hold for one to five minutes, breathing together deeply.

Results: Lying on top of her partner provides pressure against her clitoris. The partner in the Fish Pose becomes sexually invigorated from the position, with their heart chakra opening. Both partners feel connected through the heart, transferring energy and upper-body warmth.

◀ POSE 2.3: *Clitoral Stimulation and Genital Pressure*

Her position: She is in Bridge Pose (Setu Bandha), lying on her back with her arms at her sides, knees bent and feet placed flat on the floor or bed, hip-width apart. With your chin about a fist's distance from your chest, lift your lower back, interlacing your fingers together underneath it.

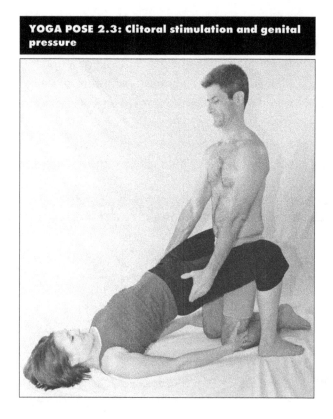

YOGA POSE 2.3: Clitoral stimulation and genital pressure

Her partner's position: Her partner is kneeling between her legs, facing her. With your hips pressed against hers, pull her pelvis upward, supporting her upper buttocks with your hands as she leans back.

Hold for up to two minutes, breathing deeply.

Results: This position opens her heart center, releasing bottled-up emotions and unwanted stress, as well as providing pressure against her clitoris and buttocks.

For those who love the clit, stimulating it never becomes old. To shake things up a bit, try shaving her pubic hair for more direct stimulation; tying bows in her pubes to give the area a new look; wearing a garter belt, thigh-highs, and crotchless panties; using edible underwear; or ducking under her long skirt, taking her G-string off with your teeth, and shaking your hair against her vulva as things get really hot down there! The more ways you learn to stimulate the clitoris, the better. Make a mental note of all of the things we covered in this chapter since they're going to come in extra handy in Chapter 14, when you learn how to help her cum in several different positions.

Her Vaginal Hot Spots for Orgasmic Eruption

During sexual arousal, a woman's vaginal walls fill with blood, causing the outer third of her vagina to swell and throb with desire. Likewise, the urethral sponge, a cluster of erectile tissue surrounding the urethra, becomes engorged with blood and swells during sexual excitement. As the urethral sponge bulges, becoming firmer, the much sought-after "Holy Grail" of hot spots—the **Gräfenberg spot**, or **G-spot**, named after its original researcher, Dr. Ernest Gräfenberg—comes to life (see Figure 3.1). This priceless pleasure trove consists of a small mass of spongy erectile nerve tissue, paraurethral ducts and glands, and blood vessels, all located between the pubic bone and the front of the cervix—about two inches in from the vaginal opening on the front (stomach) side of the vagina. The size of the tissue and the paraurethral glands it contains vary from woman to woman, but in its unaroused state it is typically the size of a pea. When stimulated effectively, it becomes prominent, enlarging to about the size of a half dollar. The sensitive G-spot does not lie directly on the vaginal wall but can be felt *through* it, in the center or slightly to the left or right of the center.

FIGURE 3.1: The internal female genitalia

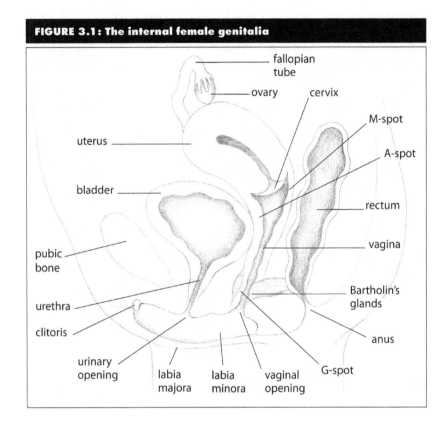

Why Is the G-Spot One of the Hottest of the Hot Spots?

The G-spot's appeal is twofold. First, as a woman goes through the sexual-response cycle, this erogenous area becomes charged by one of the most powerful nerves in the body, the pelvic nerve, which is connected to the bladder, uterus, urethra, female prostate (another name for the G-spot), PC muscle, and uterine muscles. Compared to the clitoris, its pleasure release is not nearly as concentrated or as quick to peak. This spot's erotic sensations simmer for some time when stimulated during sex play, leisurely reaching a boiling point before suddenly "rocking" a woman's entire reproductive system with muscle spasms that penetrate her core being, leading to an explosive orgasmic eruption.

Furthermore, having the G-spot massaged on a regular basis can increase genital blood flow when a woman experiences sexual arousal. This can lead to new sensations, helping some women to climax who may have been unable to do so before. Many women describe their reaction to G-spot stimulation as a powerful flushing feeling that spreads throughout both the genitals and the entire body. When the G-spot is stimulated simultaneously with the clitoris, words can't do the experience justice, but it's something like a can't-catch-my-breath, paralyzed-in-paradise state of mind, a melting-into-my-lover-while-being-launched-into-the-cosmos experience. As if these responses weren't enough, G-spot stimulation is also one more way to attain multiple orgasms and to stay sexually charged over an extended period of time. Plus, it adds more natural lubrication to the whole affair, often resulting in female ejaculation for some women.

Second, the frenzy about the G-spot—the what-is-it, where-is-it, why-can't-I-find-it, does-it-really-exist media mayhem—has turned this spot into a bit of a mystical deity. Worshipped for its unexplainable, breathtaking powers, the G-spot has caused lovers everywhere to be labeled sexual winners or losers for having found it or not. Tabloids have made locating the G-spot the ultimate crusade of lovemaking, so a certain attitude of "I'm normal," "I'm sexual," and/or "I'm an amazing lover" exists around finding it.

G-Spot Myths and Misconceptions

Myth: The G-spot doesn't exist.
Many women can attest that the G-spot *is* a hot spot that exists. And many researchers, like Drs. Alice K. Ladas, Beverly Whipple, and John D. Perry, authors of the infamous *The G Spot,* consider the G-spot an actual, responsive part of a woman's physiology—a type of female "prostate," because it consists of a group of sexually sensitive lubricating glands along the urethra, similar to the male's prostate.

Myth: All women have an erogenous G-spot; some people just have trouble finding it.
Although every woman has a G-spot, it is not an erogenous zone for every woman. Some women simply don't get anything out of having this area stimulated or don't find its reactions anything special (the same is true of all of the hot spots). Many women and couples have been made to feel

sexually challenged and incompetent because they've been chasing a treasure chest that simply doesn't hold gold for her. However, she (and her partner) is no less sexual or sexually accomplished because of this.

Myth: The G-spot produces instant magic-button reactions.
Many women and couples shoot themselves in the foot when trying to find the G-spot because they're under the impression that, once hit, this erotic area will unleash the sexual forces of the universe, blowing her away into a state of sexual satiation she's never known. The G-spot doesn't provide instant results. First, you need to take the time needed to get a woman sexually aroused, and then you need to explore the vaginal canal, again taking your time to stimulate the area. With time and patience, you may discover superpower sensations and feel like a superhero for having done so—just don't expect yourself (or her) to react with the speed of Wonder Woman.

Myth: Every woman ejaculates fluid when aroused.
While many women experience female ejaculation, especially at climax during G-spot stimulation, not every woman does. What was once a *faux pas* reaction to sexual excitement has become the "latest" in sexual response, with many women now feeling pressured to be ejaculators by proponents for the cause and partners alike. It's wonderful that this natural bodily reaction is no longer being stigmatized and is actually being supported, but we need to remember that there's great beauty in the diverse reactions we humans have to sexual stimulation. As with all other experiences, a woman is no more or less sexual, no more or less feminine, because she does or doesn't ejaculate. Such erotic potential, however, is certainly well worth exploring.

G-Spot Orgasm

G-spot orgasms, also referred to as **vaginal, internal,** or **uterine orgasms,** are triggered by G-spot stimulation and involve contractions of the whole uterus, vagina, and pelvic region. They tend to feel deeper, trigger more of an emotional reaction than clitoral orgasms, and last longer. Many women find them more relaxing and satisfying, because they produce warm waves of an "I'm-turning-to-putty" sensation that pump steadily throughout the body, making the woman feel like she's suspended in a charged, uncontrollable, climactic high.

> *You may notice that the term "uterine orgasm" is used again in the following chapter. This is because some experts hold that such orgasms are different from what is typically referred to as the G-spot orgasm. Rather than weigh in on the debate, I thought I'd keep both camps happy and let you decide what you want to call it.*

Being able to stimulate the G-spot at the same time as the clitoris can lead to a **"blended" orgasm,** which involves both the pudendal and pelvic nerves, hence the stronger reaction that includes contractions of the PC muscle. Such an orgasm is often described as more sudden, more explosive, "deeper," and longer lasting; in essence, it combines the reactions of the two types of orgasms. This is the result of internal uterine and pelvic (mostly in the outer third of the vagina) contractions. Women also generally experience feelings of deeper physical and emotional satisfaction with a blended orgasm. It should also be noted that apnea, a temporary cessation of breathing, is not as common during a blended orgasm as with a vaginal orgasm.

Rules for G-Spot Play

✳ Before attempting to stimulate the G-spot, make sure that the woman is sexually aroused, with the vagina well lubricated, so that the urethral sponge swells and becomes more noticeable to the touch. This will make it *way* easier to find.

✳ If you're using a diaphragm for birth control, reconsider. Diaphragms have been known to interfere with G-spot stimulation.

✳ Take your time finding and stimulating the G-spot, and do so on multiple occasions. This type of sexual pleasuring takes practice and perseverance, and you'll get better every time you try. You may not arouse a reaction from this spot the first time or two, or you may not do so effectively. As long as it's a hot spot, however, you'll hit the jackpot sooner or later.

❋ Make sure your fingernails are well groomed. This is not an area to scratch! Long nails should ideally be covered by latex gloves.

❋ Make sure the bladder is empty before stimulation. A woman may experience the urge to urinate when the G-spot is first stimulated but can rest assured that this is not the case if she's hit the loo (bathroom) beforehand. After no more than ten seconds of massaging, the "need-to-pee" feeling is replaced by pure sexual pleasure.

❋ Use lube! Getting things wet, or even wetter, down there will assist efforts.

❋ Make sure you're both relaxed and that this is not a goal-oriented sexpedition, even though it's hard not to look at it that way. This is about having fun, feeling sexual, exploring the body, and finding out how to make it feel good. Plan your sexploration as though going on vacation. You have a general road map of places you'd like to visit, but you are willing to get detoured and are open to new surprises that might pop up along the way. You may have such a good time in your travels that you never need to get to your destination, or you may end up arriving via ways you never imagined!

❋ Communicate with your partner. Find out what feels good. Ask her if she's aroused enough, if more pressure is needed, or if one motion feels better than another. Keep this light, sexy, and fun.

❋ Women, explore on your own. Masturbating is a perfect opportunity to take your time exploring your genitals, your hot spots, what turns you on, and how to turn you on. Get to know your G-spot and have no fear in giving a sexual show-and-tell with your partner. It's a complete win-win situation and conveys a sexual confidence that is hot.

How to Find the G-Spot

In trying to find the G-spot by herself, a woman can squat, though it is much more comfortable to sit and lean back onto a support. If with a partner, she can lie on her stomach, legs apart, with her hips slightly elevated, perhaps on a pillow. Her lover can then use two or three fingers, palm down, to apply light, then firm, pressure downward onto the vagina's anterior (front) wall (the one closer to the bed or floor). Lying on her back is also an option (and one that is commonly illustrated in sex books), with or without a pillow under the buttocks, with knees bent and legs spread; however, finding the G-spot may be much more difficult in this position. If attempting this position, the inserted fingers should be curved upward, like a fishhook, and pressure applied with a "come hither" motion.

1. Once the woman is aroused, insert two or three well-lubed fingers. Using more than one finger covers more ground and provides more stimulation. One finger can be used if she's uncomfortable and "tight," though this is often a good indication that she's not aroused enough for vaginal stimulation. Consider taking things back a step with more kissing, sharing an erotic magazine, or running your hands all over her body while telling her how irresistibly sexy she is.

2. Feel along the front vaginal wall for a rough patch about two inches in from the vaginal opening (see Figure 3.1 on page 35). You're looking for a swollen, puckering, wrinkly area, different from the surrounding soft tissue, ranging from the size of a small bean to that of a half dollar. Keep in mind that you're likelier to find it in the shallow versus deep end of the vagina. Don't bypass it by trying to stick your whole finger in, as some people do, missing the spot entirely.

3. If you're still having trouble finding the G-spot, with your other hand trace a line from the belly button to the top of the pubic bone, and with your palm or fingers gently press on the area where the pubic hairline starts. This stimulates the spot from the outside, so pressure can be applied from two angles. Shifting positions—for example, sitting up or leaning back even more—may also make it easier to find.

4. Check in with your partner. How does everything feel to her? What does she need more of? Or less of?

5. Once you feel the rough patch of the G-spot, stroke the area, using firm, deep pressure. Continue to do so in a rhythmic circular or

up-down motion, making sure to stay steady and firm. The middle finger is especially good for providing steady, rhythmic pressure, whether accompanied by the index or ring finger.

6. Continue checking in with your partner to learn what type of stimulation feels best to her. Do you need to apply more pressure? Which motion does she like best?

7. Once you're golden, gradually increase the rhythm, creating a lot of friction, which will increase the chances of having a Big O.

8. Simultaneously work other hot spots that have proven to be erotic for her, like her inner thighs or nipples, helping her to achieve more of a total-body reaction.

Finger Action for G-Spot Pleasure

❦ **EXERCISE 3.1**: *The "G" (as in Give-Me-More-of-That) Spot*

When experimenting with G-spot stimulation, consider any of the following moves:

✳ Thrust your fingers in and out of the vagina, exerting pressure upward to stimulate the G-spot when withdrawing

✳ Simultaneously stimulate the clitoris with the hand or tongue

✳ Slowly slide your fingers rhythmically from side to side across the G-spot, applying the most pressure with your middle finger

✳ Rock your fingers from side to side across the spot, always using a firm touch

✳ Gently but firmly squeeze the G-spot

❦ TIPS ❦

Let go.

Don't try to be in control as you're being pleasured, even if you're the one in charge. This acts as a resistance to your orgasmic response. Relax the same way you would at a hair salon while your head is being kneaded during a good shampooing: Close your eyes, relax, and savor the sensations, wishing you could have somebody pamper you like this every day. Look at G-spot stimulation and orgasmic response the same way—allow yourself to get sucked into the moment instead of thinking about what's going on and worrying about how you should be reacting.

Move!

Don't expect your fingers or your partner to do all the work. Simply lying there isn't going to help your cause. Get into it, especially as things start to feel good; doing so gives off nonverbal signals that your lover is making some progress. For example, move your pelvis so that it makes better contact with the fingers during stimulation.

Don't forget the clit.

Stimulate your own if you're masturbating, or, if you're the pleasuring partner, have her stimulate her own clitoris with a hand or sex toy while the G-spot is being attended to. This will help her arousal level, making her even likelier to react to G-spot efforts.

Fantasize!

Get lost in fantasy as your G-spot is being stimulated. Pretend that you're having sex with your favorite star, or pretend that you're a star and your lover is a fan willing to do anything for you, or pretend that you've been made a sex slave and your love can do whatever they want to you. This will help you take the focus off the spot and relieve you of any pressure to find it. In diverting your attention elsewhere, you may find your nether regions suddenly pulling you into a terrific O!

Bring in the reinforcements.

Try using a dildo or G-spot vibrator, especially if you're having difficulty locating and stimulating the spot or simply want more stimulation. Toys also help when your fingers tire or you need a break.

Be a terrible tease.

Go back and forth between the clitoris and G-spot, bringing each to the edge of orgasm, until you or your lover can no longer stand the sexual tension.

Try strength training.

Practice strengthening your pelvic-floor muscles (see Chapter 4). Doing so will maximize your G-spot's response, making it more sensitive and giving you more control over your orgasmic reaction. The sexual enhancers covered in Chapter 13 will help you work this area of the body even more.

Acupressure Points

◀ EXERCISE 3.2: *For More "Ohmigod" Gasps*

You can hit acupressure points at the same time that you're stimulating the G-spot. Place your other hand or your mouth over her lower abs, massaging or kissing this area with light pressure to stimulate the three Sea of Intimacy acupressure points that are located between her belly button and pubic bone. They are located two, three, and four finger-widths below the navel (see Figure 3.2). Stimulating the area right below her navel will also help to send energy to her sacral chakra, nurturing her reproductive system and cultivating more energy throughout her body. Considered the center of the human body by the ancient Chinese because the inner meridians that originate in the genitals pass through this area, these points are believed to restore, secure, and supplement sexual intimacy when stimulated.

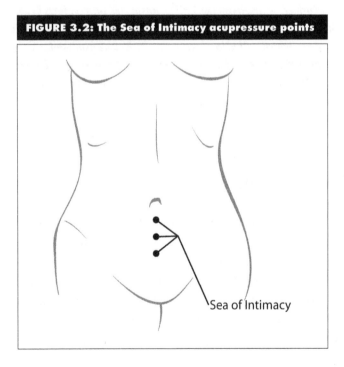

FIGURE 3.2: The Sea of Intimacy acupressure points

Sea of Intimacy

Fisting

Beyond finger action is fisting action, where one partner gradually puts their entire hand into the vagina. (This can also be done to the rectum.) Whether the hand is made into a fist or the fingers are straight and/or overlapped (not curled), this is an activity that should not be attempted unless it is done safely and properly, and preferably with an experienced partner. For those who find this sex act enjoyable, it can be a very intense, pleasurable feeling for both the giver and receiver. Fisting can, however, cause severe tissue damage and pain. Although it requires a great deal of trust, communication, relaxation, and patience—and tons of lubricant—fisting is one way some women fulfill the desire they have to be completely "filled up."

Sexual Health Considerations

To help protect yourself from sexually transmitted infections (STIs) when stimulating the G-spot or other parts of the vagina, consider wearing a latex glove, which will help to reduce the risk of transmission. Although manual-stimulation activities are considered low-risk sexual behaviors for infections like HIV, there is a chance of transmission when vaginal fluid comes into contact with any cuts or sores on the hands.

The A-Spot

The **A-spot**, or **anterior fornix erogenous (AFE) zone**, is the area on the front wall of the vagina midway between the cervix and G-spot (see Figure 3.1 on page 35). It plays a role in vaginal lubrication. Felt as a spongy, wrinkled swelling, the A-spot is so sensitive to stimulating touch that a special technique was developed to help women who experience vaginal dryness during sex, though couples who simply desire more natural vaginal lubrication can benefit from its practice as well. Some couples can also benefit from yet another of this hot spot's perks: The combination of vaginal lubrication and the A-spot's erotic sensitivity can result in orgasm(s) in some women!

To engage in the following exercise, a woman should be sitting down, leaning back on a support, with her legs bent and pulled in toward her body. Or she can squat. For optimal results, this technique should be practiced for five to ten minutes every day for at least one week.

❧ EXERCISE 3.3: *The AFE-Zone Stimulation Technique*

1. Making sure that she is aroused enough for comfortable penetration, insert one of your index fingers all the way into the vagina.

2. Gently, rhythmically, and patiently, stroke the inner, upper half of the front vaginal wall. Using a circular motion, whether clockwise or counterclockwise, may be more lucrative. You'll know your efforts are paying off as she begins to get wetter and wetter.

3. As she becomes more lubricated, bring your finger out a little way to stroke both the G-spot and the AFE zone. Use a long, repeated, thrusting motion, moving up and down the entire length of the vaginal wall, for the best results.

*Stroking the **posterior fornix zone** (PFZ), opposite and up from the AFE zone in the vaginal canal ("posterior" means "back"), may also yield pleasurable results in some women.*

Female Ejaculation

Considered just a few years ago to be incompatible with "ladylike" sexual response, the activation of a woman's waterworks during sex has become a much-sought-after, highly arousing experience for both women and their partners. What used to repulse lovers as apparent urine has been alchemized into a love potion. This transformation has occurred as education and inspiration have encouraged lovers to explore whether or not a woman's body can be trained to emit fluid during sex (if she doesn't already do so automatically).

Female ejaculation, a centuries-old phenomenon that happens in some women as a result of G-spot stimulation, occurs when a scentless, prostatic-like fluid ("ambrosia") is expelled near or during orgasm. Not to be confused with A-spot lubrication, the release of fluid (mostly through the urethra) that occurs with stimulation of the urethral sponge is likened to an actual ejaculation. It is a perfectly normal bodily response that may happen every time a woman experiences great sexual arousal and/or sexual climax (especially G-spot orgasm), some of the time, or never.

Because of its respected role in female ejaculation, tantric practitioners refer to the G-spot as the Sacred Gate.

Every woman has the potential to ejaculate. Some women and their partners know it happens, others mistake it for urination, while still others remain completely uninformed about the phenomenon. The amount of fluid ejaculated may range from a few drops to as much as 1½ cups and is determined by various factors, such as a woman's comfort in ejaculating, where she is in her menstrual cycle, the type and amount of stimulation she's receiving, and the strength of her pelvic-floor muscles. As described in Deborah Sundahl's *Female Ejaculation and the G-Spot,* female ejaculate may be salty or light and earthy in smell and taste, or have a faint smell and taste of urine, or be entirely scentless and tasteless.

Part of the reason why female ejaculation was considered so undesirable in earlier modern times was due to the great debate over what the fluid is and where it comes from. While a woman may accidentally expel urine when pushing during sex, for many this is not the case. Many, like researchers Belzer, Whipple, Moser, Zaviacic, and Cabello-Santamaria, believe that it is a prostatic fluid (like that released from the male's prostate) that contains glucose, fructose, prostate-specific antigen, and the primary markers of urine (very low levels of creatinine and urea), and that it is expelled into the urethral canal by the forty or so glands and ducts of the female prostate. One more recent study by Dr. Gary Schubach involving seven women found that the 50–900 ml. of fluid expelled unquestionably came from their bladders, despite the fact that they had been drained prior to sexual arousal. When analyzed, the fluid was found to be a greatly reduced concentration of two primary components in urine, urea and creatinine, in many ways complementing previous research. The possible presence of a milky-white fluid from the urethral glands and ducts was observed as well. Researchers concluded that the fluid came from a combination of residual moisture in the walls of the bladder and from postdrainage kidney output, as well as possibly an emission of the urethral glands and ducts.

Many people consider female ejaculation highly arousing, regardless of the fluid's makeup or source. Part of being okay with the phenomenon involves normalizing it, becoming more educated about it, and understanding that it is a perfectly natural reaction to sexual excitement. Talking to your partner can help to diffuse some of the embarrassment and ignorance surrounding the issue—such as may arise, for example, from thinking she's just lost the contents of her bladder—and can show that you're sexually empowered and confident. Furthermore, explaining that it's a reaction to how aroused you are will make it a form of flattery more than anything else.

Whether or not your (or your lover's) G-spot is sensitive, your A-spot assists in lubrication, or you're a female ejaculator, what's important to take away from this chapter is that every woman is unique. Every woman will react differently to various kinds of stimulation of her internal hot spots and will also react differently from one time to the next. As you explore the full potential of the G-spot and the A-spot, don't put pressure on yourself or your lover to react in a certain way. Your body will do what it's meant to do naturally, and being able to embrace that reality will make sex play much more pleasurable for both of you.

Her Undiscovered,
Make-Me-Moan Spots

The clitoris, mons pubis, inner lips, outer lips, urethral opening, and vaginal opening together make up what is referred to as the **vulva**, or **pudendum**, the female's external genitals (see Figure 4.1). This is a highly erogenous area that protects the vagina. We've already reviewed the clitoris, but the erotic potential held in the vulva's other parts are well worth exploring since the results can be absolutely out of this world, depending on your partner's preferences and the types of stimulation that take her breath away.

Even though they are part of a female's internal genitalia, two other hot spots are covered in this chapter: the cervix and the M-spot. They are featured here because, had I included them in the last chapter, they may have gotten overlooked during the excitement that comes from talking about the G-spot, and because, like the other erogenous zones covered in this chapter, they're often ignored starlets, bursting with unrealized talent and just waiting to be discovered.

FIGURE 4.1: The external female genitalia (vulva)

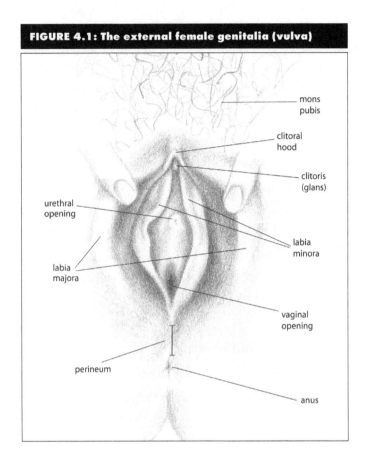

- mons pubis
- clitoral hood
- clitoris (glans)
- urethral opening
- labia minora
- labia majora
- vaginal opening
- perineum
- anus

Vulval Myths and Misconceptions

Myth: Only the clitoris has orgasmic potential.

Playing solely with any of the body parts described in this chapter may result in an orgasm—or several, for that matter. You should keep in mind that reactions vary from person to person, so don't be disappointed if stimulation of any of these spots doesn't do anything for you. Toying with the clitoris at the same time, however, will increase the chances of orgasmic response when stimulating any area of the body.

Myth: Women can only have one of three kinds of orgasm— clitoral, vaginal, or a blend of the two.

While many women may typically experience clitoral, vaginal, and/or blended orgasms, stimulation of other parts of the body, including the other areas of her vulva and her internal genitals, may result in a much different orgasmic experience. It is limiting to think that any human being can only have a certain type of orgasm. Like any potential aphrodisiac, the second you believe that something is sexual or that you will have a certain reaction to it, you are likelier to elicit the very response you desire.

Rules for Vulval Play

✳ Begin stimulation with slow, light touches, especially if you're not sure what she likes. The vulval area is made up of tender, sensitive tissue and needs to be treated accordingly. If she likes it rougher, by all means, oblige.

✳ Get it wet. As she gets more and more turned on, dip your fingers into her vagina, as if you were finger painting, to obtain her own natural secretions for use on the vulva. If she's having a dry day, the use of other lubes, like K-Y's Warming Jelly, can result in a vaginal-area slip'n'slide and can also heat things up by creating tingly sensations.

✳ It practically goes without saying at this point, but make sure your fingernails are smooth and free of hangnails, and be sure to use lube, if necessary.

⊲ TIPS ⊳

Try different moves.

With any of these hot spots, take several shots at stimulating one over several intimate engagements. Different sensations may produce different reactions at different moments. For example, see if she prefers continuous, persistent caresses or more repeated, stop-and-go movements. Keep in mind that she may have a totally different response after a long day's work, when she's in need of much doting, than she will late on a Sunday morning, when she's feeling frisky after a good night's sleep. One area may be much more sensitive right before or during her period, whereas she may get totally turned on in a different way when she's pregnant and her genitals are more engorged with blood. This being the case, you should always ask her how she's feeling, letting her know that you're there to meet her every need. All she has to do is keep you informed!

Barer may be better.

Try shaving (e.g., landing-strip style) or giving the vulval area a close trim, perhaps working in the actual process of hair removal as a part of foreplay. This will create a much different, "smoother" reaction when fooling around, and it can lead to stimulation even when she is simply walking around (less hair means her clothes will rub against her groin more intimately, adding a whole new element to foreplay). Plus, shaving will help women who have issues with pubic hair or genital cleanliness feel more comfortable during sex.

"You likey?"

Ask for feedback to help you adjust your speed and pressure so that she's getting the most out of your adoration of her.

Plant a seed.

Start a conversation ahead of time about the nonclitoral parts of her genitals. For example, ask, "Have you ever had your vaginal lips played with?" or, "Do you like pressure against your cervix during thrusting?" or, "What gets you off down there besides your clitoris?" Many people are ignorant about the erogenous potential of even their own various body parts. Having been taught that only certain areas produce specific results, they tune out a potential hot spot's erotic qualities, becoming dismissive when sex play doesn't involve the stars of the show. As we've seen on many hit television series, like *Cheers* and *Will and Grace,* it is often the supporting cast, and not the main characters, that make the show worth tuning in to time and time again. So planting the seed for sexploration possibilities can help your lover become more receptive and open-minded about what it is you're striving for when stimulating her in a certain way, and may let her know that she could be in for a surprisingly rousing reaction. Talking to your partner not only invites you both to learn more about each other's sexual likes and dislikes, but it can also challenge your expectations under the sheets. If a person doesn't expect to get turned on by a certain move, this thought could in and of itself foil your boudoir efforts. So go ahead and counter such self-fulfilling prophecies!

Mons Pubis

The **mons pubis,** a.k.a. **mons veneris,** is the fatty pad of tissue covering her pubic bone in the area where she sports pubic hair (if she hasn't shaved). All too often ignored, this area, full of nerve endings, can be an erogenous zone if manipulated properly. Rubbing and stroking the mons can indirectly stimulate her clitoris. This is especially effective if you're holding her and manually stimulating her from behind. Also, take a few moments during sex play to simply cup and hold the mons. Like a guy who finds comfort in holding his genitals, often unconsciously, having her mons area gently held can provide her with a calming, reassuring feeling. Using fingers to apply pressure on the mons area during intimacy can also enhance her orgasm; in particular, circular massaging motions can kick things up a notch.

◀ EXERCISE 4.1: *Ahhhhhh!*

With one hand firmly resting on either her mons or over her entire vulva, place your other hand over her heart or one breast. (It may be easiest to do this while holding her from behind.) Using visualization, inhale energy from her chest area, and then exhale it onto her genital area. Imagine your hands and body acting as conductors as you draw energy from her heart and send it to her vulva. The deliberate use of breath, in turn, will add passionate energy to the firm touch that you use on her vulva. After doing these actions for a while, tap on the mons area to create another wave of energy.

U-Spot

Depending on the source, the U-spot refers to either the urethral sponge or the **urethral opening**, the protrusion between a woman's clitoris and vaginal opening that expels urine (see Figure 4.1 on page 49). Since we covered the urethral sponge in our discussion of the G-spot, here we're going to focus exclusively on the urethral opening's erogenous potential. Because it is filled with nerve endings, the urethral opening can be a hot spot in some women when gently stimulated either before, during, or after orgasm; however, many women find such stimulation unpleasant or uncomfortable, or they feel nothing at all. Some women find the U-spot more sensitive when their bladder is nearly full.

For women who are into this erogenous zone, the urethral opening becomes a raised nub when stimulated, possibly changing position slightly due to preorgasmic muscle contractions. An orgasm brought about by stimulation of the U-spot (what some people call a uterine orgasm) tends to be quieter than other types, but when the area is stimulated along with the G-spot, the resulting orgasm can be mind-blowing, often resulting in female ejaculation. To arouse this area, use lubricant, and circle, rub, or press the U-spot with your fingers or a sex toy, making sure to gauge whether or not what you are doing feels good to your lover.

Labia Majora and Labia Minora

A woman's labia consist of two parts. The **outer lips** (**labia majora**) are the rounded pads of fatty tissue that lie on either side of the vaginal entrance. Covered with pubic hair, they also contain sebaceous glands and sweat glands, which produce an odorous perspiration that is a natural pheromone of sorts. The **inner lips** (**labia minora**) are thin folds of skin, usually a bit damp, that lie between the outer lips and the vaginal entrance, extending forward to meet at the front of the clitoris and form the clitoral hood.

Labia vary from woman to woman in color and shape, with some women having more pronounced inner lips. (For this reason, some people take issue with the use of the terms "majora" and "minora," which, in Latin, literally mean "larger" and "smaller.") They may be gray, pale pink, or dark, ranging from thin and narrow to thick and fleshy—and they are often not symmetrical, which is counter to what many pornography magazines would have you believe. One side may be different from the other—for example, hanging lower—especially as the woman becomes aroused and the lips are engorged with blood. Both lips are extremely sensitive to touch, especially the inner ones, with some women finding this area even more erotic than their clitoris. When stimulated, the inner lips swell and grow puffy due to increased blood circulation, eventually opening for further arousal and possible vaginal penetration.

The vulval lips are a playground for sex moves. They can be stroked, kneaded, nibbled, caressed, fondled, teased, pushed, or licked. You can give them joint attention (for example, by pressing both lips together for a massage with your thumbs), or you can give them individual attention (for example, by using your fingertips to quickly circle up the inner labia to the clitoris and back down again). Other moves may include pressing the outer lips together with your index fingers and pulling them upward, cupping the labia with your hands and rubbing them together, or blowing air onto them. (Note: *Do not* blow into the vagina, especially if a woman is pregnant, as this could cause an embolism—a blood clot in an artery—and lead to death.)

✒ EXERCISE 4.2: *Seventh-Heaven Stimulation*

1. Stroke the area where her groin and thigh meet on one side, going as far as her mons pubis before stroking along the other side. Do this several times, slowly and sensually, so that she feels the energy moving around her pelvis.

2. As if you have all the time in the world, trace the outer lips with your fingertips, lightly tickling them, absorbing what they feel like.

3. Massage and caress the outer lips with long, sweeping strokes, occasionally applying pressure to the area between the outer lips and thighs.

4. If she has pubic hair, pull it or twirl it in your fingers to indirectly stimulate the outer labia.

5. Mimic step 3, but this time using your tongue.

6. Work your way to the inner lips, starting at the vaginal opening. Use the tip of your tongue to make short, left-right motions moving up and down each lip, varying the pressure according to what feels good to her. Continue to do this, but without hitting the clitoris. See what reactions are provoked when you just focus on the lips.

7. With your hands, work other parts of her body—her nipples, her waist, the area where her buttocks and legs meet—as you lick her inner lips as if you were licking an ice cream cone. For "poetic emphasis," as you reach the top of the inner lips, give them a firm flick, much like the tongue motion you'd make when taking ice cream into your mouth.

P-Spot

Found in both sexes, the **perineum (P-spot)** is the soft tissue between the vaginal opening and the anus that is composed of spongy erectile tissue and nerve endings, and it is where many pelvic-floor muscles crisscross each other (see Figure 4.1 on page 49). Connected to the pudendal nerve, it is a huge hot spot, especially in men, which is why it is given separate attention for males in Chapter 6. In tantric practice, the perineum is the area that houses, and releases, the energy of the root chakra, which, if allowed to uncoil along the length of the spine, provides wisdom and enlightenment. Referred to as Hui-Yin in acupressure, meaning the Gate of Life and Death, it is a point vital to sexual practice and reflexology, and it is related to female sexual desire. The point can be pressed for four seconds with the fingertips, released, and pressed again; do this up to forty times or for five minutes as a way to help enhance her orgasm, relieve pressure on her genitals and rectum, and create benefits for her reproductive system.

There are a number of ways the perineum can be stimulated in females. A woman herself can pull it upward as she inhales, using the same pelvic-floor muscles she uses to stop her stream of urine. This strengthens and activates her vaginal opening, making penetration even more arousing. For some women, it feels good if you press the perineum with the heel of your hand, especially while stimulating other hot spots with your fingers. The perineum can also be stretched, helping to elongate the clitoris and maximize its orgasmic potential. This is because the action causes the clitoral hood to retract, allowing for more friction and increased sensitivity. Yet another way to stimulate the perineum is to pinch it from both sides with your thumb and index finger.

For women who are skeptical about anal play, paying more attention to her perineum may help her to feel like she's doing something almost anal and racy without violating any concerns she has about anal penetration.

⬛ EXERCISE 4.3: *The Kivin Method*

Formulated by Dr. Patti Britton, the **Kivin Method** (a.k.a. Tahitian oral-sex technique) utilizes the female's perineum, providing a deeper orgasm with a perineum-clitoris connection. As you're stimulating her orally, slowly sweep your tongue back and forth over the hood of her clitoris, feeling for two tiny bumps on each side of her clitoral hood. As you're doing this, keep two fingers on either side of the hood. Slowly increase your speed, maintaining your stroke. With your other hand, gently press your middle finger into her perineum. As she nears climax, sweep your tongue across the head of her clitoris and continue through her orgasms. Note: This method is best done while a woman is on her back, her partner perpendicular and approaching her from a right angle. The key, as well, is paying attention to her responses. You may need to adjust your tongue speed.

Vaginal Weight Lifting

All Eastern approaches to sex teach about the importance of exercising the pubococcygeus muscle in order to increase circulation of blood and sexual hormones to the brain center. This is because in both sexes all of the body's major meridians, which carry energy between the vital organs, pass through the pelvic-floor area. If these muscles are blocked or weak, energy will dissipate and organs will suffer. Pelvic-floor exercises help to strengthen the reproductive organs and the area's tendons, help the tissues to communicate with all other parts of the body, and help to maintain overall health. For women, such exercises are sometimes referred to as "Kegel" exercises, after the Western doctor who developed them.

The "pubococcygeus muscle," or "PC muscle," is a collective term for the group of pelvic-floor muscles that stretch from the pelvic bone to the tailbone, encircling the base of the vagina (or penis), the urethra, and the rectum. The muscles contract naturally during orgasm, partly because the pudendal nerve, which detects most genital and anal stimulation, runs through them, triggering most of their reactions and sending and receiving arousal messages to and from the brain.

Known to increase sexual desire, sensation, and sexual pleasure; intensify and produce more orgasms; and help one become multiorgasmic, the pelvic-floor muscles are more responsive when better toned. The following exercise helps the vagina to feel tighter to both the woman and her partner, whether she's being stimulated by a finger, penis, or sex toy. Perhaps one of the greatest benefits of a toned PC muscle is increased sexual self-confidence. To feel the contractions, place your finger on your perineum as you do the exercise.

❦ EXERCISE 4.4: *Basic PC Toning*

1. Empty your bladder.

2. Identify the PC muscle by using the same muscles that stop the flow of your urine stream.

3. Squeeze them tightly for three to ten seconds, with the goal being to eventually hold the contraction for a full ten seconds.

4. Release.

5. Repeat ten times. Do up to three sets of ten reps per day.

You can alter this exercise by doing fast contractions—tightening and relaxing the muscles as rapidly as possible, yet still using control—for ten seconds.

Kabazzah is an Eastern sexual skill, often a part of tantric practice, wherein a woman mounts a man and then moves only her internal muscles to bring him to climax while he does nothing more than stay relaxed.

Using a stone or crystal egg (not a real egg) can help you to further strengthen and control your vaginal muscles. You will exercise not only your PC muscle but also your urogenital and pelvic diaphragms, further strengthening and toning the entire area and developing sexual response.

❦ EXERCISE 4.5: *Egg-cellent*

Don't try this variation until you've built up your strength with basic Kegel exercises. This exercise should be done using a stone or crystal egg.

1. Stand with your feet slightly wider than hip distance apart, knees slightly bent.

2. Insert the egg, large end first, into the vagina.

3. Contract the muscle group around your vaginal opening (this helps keep the egg from slipping out).

4. While inhaling, contract the vaginal canal muscles directly below the cervix as you simultaneously contract the lower (PC) muscles.

5. Squeeze the middle section of the vaginal canal so that you have a good grip on the egg, and then push it downward.

6. Inhale and squeeze harder, so as to slowly move the egg upward.

7. Continue with a slow and steady up-down movement, using a firm grip.

As you get better at doing this, you will gradually be able to increase the speed of this motion.

X-Spot

The X-spot refers to the **cervix,** the opening to a woman's uterus (see Figure 3.1 on page 35). It has long been considered a hot spot in Taoist tradition, which views both the cervical area and tip of the penis as corresponding to the heart. It is the interaction between these two hot spots, heterosexually speaking, that triggers pleasure. Since it has relatively few nerve endings, the cervix is more responsive to pressure than to touch; some women, especially those who have undergone multiple childbirths, find pressure applied by a penis or a sex toy arousing. On the other hand, many women have no reaction to cervical stimulation or find it downright painful, especially during hard, deep thrusting.

It is common to stimulate the cervix with the tip of the penis or with a sex toy, but lovers can also explore manually stimulating it by inserting one or more fingers into the vaginal canal and encircling the cervix. You can glide over this area with your fingertips, slowly applying pressure, with most of the direct pressure being absorbed by the palm of your hand against the mons pubis. You can also circle the X-spot with gentle little pokes, if that feels good to her.

While doing either move, place the palm of your other hand over the middle of her lower belly and apply slow, deep pressure. This will activate the Gate of Origin acupressure point, located directly above the uterine area (see Figure 4.2), as well as her sacral chakra. Let her know that you are trying to stimulate this point so she can tune into that area of her body and its energy, making the action more of a team effort. Sucking on this acupressure point will have arousing effects as well.

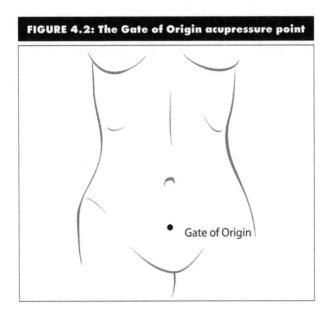

FIGURE 4.2: The Gate of Origin acupressure point

Gate of Origin

Any cervical action can trigger movement in the internal uterine wall and its broad supporting ligaments, causing radiating sensations and resulting in a **cervical orgasm**. Considered a type of **internal, vaginal,** or **uterine orgasm**, this stellar reaction is a deep, intense O, believed to emanate from the stimulation of nerves and nerve endings around the cervix and upper vaginal canal, especially in the peritoneum, the large membrane that lines the abdominal cavity.

M-Spot

The hot spot that Christa Schulte dubs the **M-spot** (as in "mmmm") in her book *Tantric Sex for Women* can only be felt after a woman has already had an orgasm. The M-spot lies just below the mouth of the uterus (see Figure 3.1 on page 35). When the vagina lifts up, forming a "roof" or "tent" of sorts, the spot can be felt at the inner peak of the tent. Most easily stimulated with a long finger or a toy and by using a constant, soft tapping or vibrating motion, this spot shoots energy to a woman's heart chakra and third eye chakra, lengthening her climactic high. Like the cervix, this hot spot can also be triggered via the Gate of Origin acupressure point.

Yoga Poses for Vulval Stimulation

❦ POSE 4.1: *Vulval and Root Chakra Stimulation*

Her position: You get into Double Wind Releasing Pose (Pavanamuktasana), lying on your back with your knees bent. Instead of hugging your knees into your chest, allow them to drop open. After your partner is on top of you, wrap your legs around them.

Her partner's position: Lie between her legs on your belly, legs straight together, toes curled under in Cobra Pose (Bhujangasana), i.e., your weight is supported by your hands and toes and your back is arched so that the crown of your head is pointing upward. Pressing your hips downward as you extend your upper body into a slightly arched backbend will stimulate her vulva.

Hold for up to one minute.

YOGA POSE 4.1: Vulval and root chakra stimulation

Results: This position stimulates her root chakra and opens both partners' heart chakras, as well as providing some pressure against the vulva.

❦ POSE 4.2: *Vulval and Penile Stimulation*

Her position: Lie on your back and pull your right leg up for Reclined Big Toe Pose (Supta Padangusthasana), grasping your calf with both hands. As you exhale, and while keeping your leg as straight as possible, hold your right big toe with the first two fingers of your right hand and gently lower your leg toward your right shoulder.

Her partner's position: Make a split over her pelvis, bringing your right leg up toward her shoulder. Lean forward to grab hold of your right big toe with the first two fingers of your right hand.

Hold for two minutes. This position can also be done using the opposite leg.

YOGA POSE 4.2: Vulval and penile stimulation

Results: Allows for more advanced sexual positions and allows for pelvis-on-vulva stimulation, especially of the perineum.

The general communication rule with all of these spots is *"Do* ask and *do* tell." Find out what feels good to her. Tell your lover if something just ain't doin' anything for you or if you think the technique needs to be changed up a little bit. Experiment with stimulating these spots with some of the toys and positions I discuss in the last two chapters of this book. By expecting the unexpected when you least expect it, you may end up pleasantly surprised.

His Hot Spots
for Explosive Results

Although I took a "ladies-first" approach in presenting the hot spots, doing so was not meant to undermine the golden potential of the male erogenous zones and everything they have to offer him and his partner. In the next three chapters, we get up close and personal with trigger areas throughout his groin and investigate all the ways a man or his lover can move mountains with just the right touch.

Few hot spots have quite the degree of symbolic meaning and clout as the penis, which has reigned as the male's hottest erogenous zone since the beginning of time, serving as a revered reflection of one's manhood and sexual prowess. Sometimes referred to as a scepter (a baton anointed by a sovereign as a symbol of authority), the penis can be a man's all-consuming pride and joy or simply regarded as his most appreciated source of pleasure for the erotic sensations it produces throughout the genitals and, at times, the entire body.

Human interest and appreciation aside, the **penis** is the very sensitive male reproductive organ that is composed of three main parts: (1) the

glans, the smooth, extremely sensitive tip, which is packed with numerous nerve endings; (2) the **body,** or **shaft,** which contains a rich network of blood vessels and spongy cylinders (a pair of corpora cavernosa and a corpus spongiosum; see Figure 6.1 on page 85) that have the potential to fill with blood and expand during erection; and (3) the **root,** which attaches to the body. In extending back into the body, the roots of the corpora cavernosa, the **crura,** attach to the surface of the ischiopubic rami, the branches of the pelvis. This structure prevents the penis from sinking into the perineum as the man's body bears the impact of thrusting.

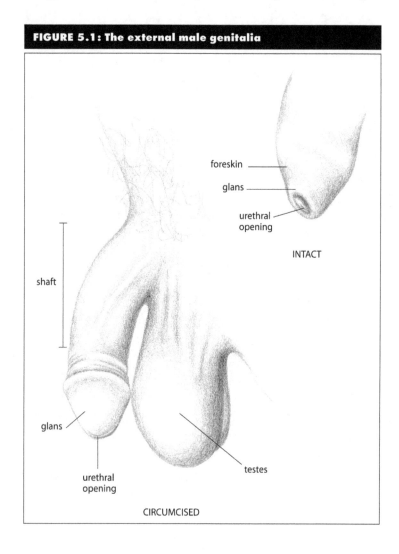

FIGURE 5.1: The external male genitalia

foreskin

glans

urethral opening

INTACT

shaft

glans

urethral opening

testes

CIRCUMCISED

Penises range in size and shape. They can be any combination of long, medium, or short in length and skinny, medium, or thick in girth. They may hang straight down or slightly toward one thigh; some erect penises point more to one side than the other. Larger flaccid (nonerect) penises do not increase as much in size during erection as do smaller flaccid penises. The average flaccid penis is 2 to 4 inches in length if measured along the underside from where the penis shaft protrudes from the groin. The average erect penis ranges in length from 4⅝ to 6¼ inches, with the average girth being 4.83 inches. Anywhere within an inch of that range is considered mainstream; 12 percent of the population exceeds it and 12 percent falls under it.

The skin of the penis may be loose prior to erection, tightening and becoming darker in color as the organ fills with blood during erection. Penises may have papules, which are natural, pearly, raised bumps that appear around the base of the glans; or Fordyce's spots, small, yellowish-white spots; and/or sebaceous prominences, which are located at the sweat glands.

One major misconception about the penis is that this magic wand is one big erogenous zone. In actuality, it is covered with several specialized, highly erotic areas, specifically, the glans, corona, frenulum, and (for most males worldwide) the foreskin (see Figure 5.1). When playing with the penis, pay attention to the following hot spots and to the exercises on how to sex them up. Knowing what you need to do and where to do it will elicit major kudos for your abilities as a lover, setting you apart from other tourists who have been under the misguided impression that the male phallus is just one big resort. Instead, know that it is full of a bunch of smaller, off-the-beaten-path, must-see locales that give this pleasure site its heart and soul.

Foreskin

All males are born with a **foreskin**, or **prepuce**, a layer of skin full of rich blood vessels, nerve endings, and muscle fibers (see Figure 5.1). This retractable, double-layered fold of skin is in fact a mucous membrane. It is a modified extension of the penile shaft's skin that covers and usually extends beyond the glans. It automatically pulls back when the male is aroused and erect. Men who are circumcised have had this highly erogenous tissue removed.

The foreskin consists of two parts: the ridged mucosa and the soft mucosa, which lies against the glans. The soft mucosa contains sebaceous glands that secrete emollients, lubricants, and protective antibodies; it acts much like an eyelid that protects the eye by cleansing and moisturizing it. Believed by many to serve a protective purpose, the foreskin keeps the glans surface soft and moist, and provides the skin necessary to accommodate an erect penis, allowing skin tissue to glide smoothly over the shaft and glans as the penis becomes thicker and is stimulated; for example, during sexual intercourse.

It is important to pull the foreskin back when putting on a condom. Otherwise, the condom could end up inside the foreskin, uncomfortably reducing sensitivity and effectiveness.

Glans

The **glans**, or head of the penis, is the extended cap of the corpus spongiosum (see Figure 6.1 on page 85) and is covered wholly or partially by the foreskin unless a man is aroused or has been circumcised (see Figure 5.1 on page 64). Extremely sensitive, the glans is usually reddish or purplish during arousal, smooth, shiny, and moist (though dry if circumcised). Data are mixed as to whether or not the glans is more sensitive in men who are uncircumcised (with a foreskin) than in those who are not. Regardless, this hot spot can send shivers up his spine when properly stimulated.

Corona

The **corona**, sometimes referred to as the **coronal ridge**, is a raised ridge located at the bottom of the glans, separating the penis's head from its shaft (see Figure 5.1). For some men, it is the most sexually excitable hot spot on the penis. In circumcised men, it is normal for the corona to have expanded to a diameter significantly greater than that of the penile shaft. Having been circumcised allows for full stimulation of the corona during sexual activity. In uncircumcised men, the corona may not be totally visible until or even during erection.

According to a recent study by DaiSik Kim & Myung-Geol Pang, following adult circumcision, many men reported a decrease in masturbatory pleasure and sexual enjoyment, indicating that getting snipped negatively affects sexual function in many men.

F-Spot

The **frenulum (F-spot)**, also called the **frenum** or **fraenum**, is a tiny, loose band of skin or a small bump located near the indentation on the underside of the penis where the glans meets the shaft (in the twelve o'clock position; see Figure 5.1 on page 64). This fibrous cord of connecting tissue joins the glans to the inner foreskin, helping to contract the foreskin over the glans. In some men, it is the most sensitive part of the penis. It can be stimulated in an up-and-down fashion with varying pressure and speed. Since most men find the F-spot to be highly sensitive to touch, its function is thought to be that of providing pleasure by stretching during sexual intercourse. In fact, some men find that they reach orgasm too quickly if the F-spot receives unusually intense stimulation during intercourse or other forms of sex.

For circumcised men, the frenulum is an extremely sensitive area of scar tissue, seen as a slight bump. Scar tissue can be more sensitive than regular skin, with penile scar tissue being even that much more sensitive.

In heterosexual sex play, a woman can stimulate her man's frenulum and her clitoris at the same time. She starts by lying on her back with her legs shut. The man squeezes his lubricated penis between her thighs, thrusting up against her vulva. Squeezing her thighs together will provide even more stimulation. This can also be done from behind in a spooning position. Slightly crossing her legs and squeezing her upper thighs around his shaft provides even greater "ohmigod" stimulation.

Among the frenulum's marvels is its role in helping men with complete spinal-cord lesions (quadriplegia) to reproduce. Since a quadriplegic cannot ejaculate during coitus, vibratory stimulation can be applied to the frenulum to produce ejaculate for intrauterine insemination.

U-Spot

The male's urethral opening, or **U-spot**, a slitlike vertical opening in the glans, is the orifice through which urine and semen are released (see Figure 5.1 on page 64). It can be an erogenous area for some men, though many find its stimulation uncomfortable, painful, or simply ineffective. To stimulate this area, use lube and gently circle, rub, or press it with your fingers or a sex toy, making sure to check in with your partner as to whether or not such arousal feels good.

Why Is the Penis One of the Hottest Spots?

The penis is lauded as the trophy of all male hot spots because it puts on one helluva show. Plus, because of its sensitivity to touch, pressure, temperature, and stimuli, it is often regarded as having a mind of its own. Among the nerves that make the penis such a major hub of erotic activity are the dorsal nerve, which is a continuation of the pudendal nerve, and the greater cavernous nerve, which is key in erection.

But what really gets "ooohs" and "ahhhs" is the penis's response to sexual stimulation. When sexually excited, a man's penis becomes erect as it fills with blood and hardens, causing the glans to swell and become more noticeable. It's practically irresistible, like an endearing puppy at the pound that locks in your gaze. It begs for attention.

Erections happen because the penis's internal structure consists of spongy erectile bodies that fill with blood and swell (the corpora cavernosa and corpus spongiosum mentioned earlier; see Figure 6.1 on page 85). As a man gets more and more turned on, a few drops of fluid, known as pre-ejaculatory fluid or pre-cum, appear at the tip of the penis. As his performance continues, he hovers near a titillating sexual boiling point for as long as he can control himself, before bursting into orgasm, most often complemented by a geyserlike show of ejaculation! (Note: A man can ejaculate without necessarily having an orgasm, and he can also have an orgasm without necessarily ejaculating.)

Penis-Induced Orgasm

For most men, orgasm is almost always attained entirely through penile stimulation—the **penis-induced orgasm**—and is almost always accompanied by the ejaculation of semen. This orgasm actually originates at his prostate, moving into his penis and testicles, seizing his entire reproductive system. The muscles at the base of the penis and urethral bulb contract rhythmically, forcing semen through the urethra and then out of the opening at the tip of the penis. In some cases, with proper breathing, mindfulness, and control, this climactic reaction can spread, becoming a total mind-body-spirit experience.

Penis Myths and Misconceptions

Myth: Penises without foreskins are better.

Functionally speaking, both circumcised and uncircumcised penises are highly erogenous. Men experience a great deal of penile sensitivity with or without their foreskin. The foreskin does, however, contain a richer variety and greater concentration of specialized nerve receptors than any other part of the penis, which is why many men who have been circumcised feel unjustly deprived of their full erotic potential. (Note: Because the foreskin is so sensitive, partners should determine whether a man prefers for his foreskin to slide over the head of the penis during sexual stimulation or for it to be pulled back. His preference will probably depend on the type of sex play he's engaging in.)

Aesthetically speaking, blessing a penis as attractive or not based on the presence or absence of a foreskin is really a matter of personal preference and of what people are used to seeing. Factors like whether or not a culture circumcises its newborns (most around the world do not), or whether illustrations and photos show circumcised or uncircumcised penises (portrayals in the United States tend to show circumcised penises), play into what is visually appealing for both men and women.

Myth: All penises like to be stimulated in the same way.

Every male is different when it comes to penile stimulation. Some prefer concentration on the glans, and others would much rather have the corona lavished with sensation. Some prefer a certain kind of stroke. And preferences can change from time to time, depending on a guy's mood, his fatigue level, the arousal situation, etc. It is important to be versatile when working with the penis and to check in with your partner about what is working for him at any particular moment.

Myth: Bigger is better.

Penis size is largely a matter of preference. Some people prefer large penises while others would opt for smaller ones during lovemaking. Different activities also make having a bigger or smaller penis more or less enjoyable or difficult. It really comes down to lovers' compatibilities, needs, and body types. Ultimately, as long as a man knows how to please his partner, stimulating their hot spots in a way that likens him to the gods, his size often becomes secondary in importance.

Myth: Masturbation affects penis size.

Masturbating does not make the penis permanently bigger or smaller.

Rules for Penis Play

✳ Make sure that your nails are well groomed, with no hangnails or rough edges.

✳ Do not scrape the penis with your teeth.

✳ Most men like a firm touch, so use strong, direct, intense stimulation —both while getting him erect and while stimulating him once he's erect. You should also ask him now and again if more or less stimulation is needed.

✳ Try varying your fondling action from time to time, recognizing that different touches may create different sensations from one sexual episode to the next. Starting out lightly with gentle, teasing touches and grazing strokes will help to build anticipation and allow both of you to ease into foreplay.

✳ Make sure he's comfortable. Having him sit up against a wall or on pillows during manual or oral stimulation will help him to feel more at ease and will make it easier for either of you to touch the entire genital area.

✳ Don't get discouraged if he loses his erection. It happens on occasion for physical, mental, or emotional reasons. Unless there's a problem in the relationship that needs to be worked out or he has a physical ailment that needs attention, this reaction is not an indication of your lack of skill in stimulating him or of his being "less of a man."

✳ Use lube generously, experimenting with various types. Some may have a more numbing effect than others—it all comes down to personal preference. In addition to water- or silicone-based lubes that have a smooth, comfortable effect, you can use your own spit or any pre-cum he emits during stimulation. Oil-based products such as baby oil and Vaseline—as well as slick, greasy lubes like Elbow Grease, ID Cream, and Boy Butter—are also options, but only if you're not going to use latex forms of protection, since oil can cause latex condoms, gloves, and dental dams to deteriorate. Oil-based products can also stain your sheets and other fabrics and are pretty hard to clean up. With the use of most oil-based lubes, the penis will need to be cleaned before penetrating the vagina, because these lubes are not good for the vagina's chemistry (this isn't a concern with plain petroleum jelly or unscented mineral oil, but be reminded that even these products break down latex barriers).

✳ Communicate with each other! Every man is unique in his likes and dislikes. What may have worked for one may not fly with this one, and only he can tell you what feels good and how things can feel even better.

✳ Masturbate! Get to know your penis if you don't already. Take the time to learn what turns you on—the pressure, stimulation, and sensations your penis reacts to—so that you can later share this info in the sack with someone special. It's good to know what your body likes under various circumstances so that you can teach your lover about your needs and can understand your reactions; for example, how your arousal and sexual-response cycle are affected after a few drinks or an intense workout.

✳ Don't get so enchanted by your own penis that you miss out on your lover's reactions to getting your motor going. Many partners love playing with the penis! Enjoy watching your lover get excited as they bring your member to life, worshipping it until you rumble with hot-spring reactions.

✳ As a courtesy, and as a safer-sex must, give your partner a heads-up that you're about to come, allowing your partner the option to spit or swallow.

✳ If you're the one being pleasured, do not force your penis deeper into your partner's mouth unless they have given you the okay to do so. This can be very uncomfortable and can make a person feel like they are choking or having an "I'm-about-to-throw-up" reaction.

Show your lover how you like to be stimulated. Then ask your partner to place their hand over yours, taking note of your rhythm, energy level, and motions. As your lover takes over, guide the hand motion if necessary, all the while offering positive or constructive feedback by saying, for example, "That feels really good. I'd love it if you could hit that spot even more."

Hand Action for Penis Pleasure

Before giving him the hand job of his life, you need to get him erect. Although there are a ton of ways you can do this—dressing up in a sexy number, whispering what you're about to do to him, or letting him play with your hottest spots first—we're going to focus here on the most direct, hands-on tactic. First, warm your lubed-up hands by rubbing them together before touching the penis. Roll the penis between your palms, as though rolling dough. Apply firm pressure with one finger midway between the base of his penis and the anus (the perineum).

◖ EXERCISE 5.1: *Ultimate Hand Job*

1. Massage his groin area, particularly the crease where the inner thigh meets the torso. This will stimulate his Rushing Door and Mansion Cottage acupressure points (see Figure 5.2).

2. Press his penis up against his belly. This move can help to indirectly stimulate his G-spot (more on this topic in Chapter 6).

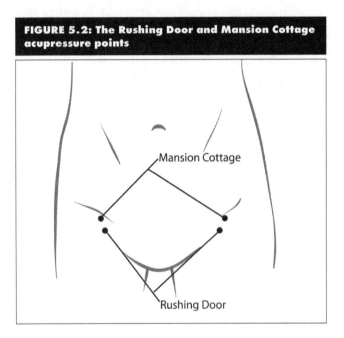

FIGURE 5.2: The Rushing Door and Mansion Cottage acupressure points

Mansion Cottage

Rushing Door

3. Using one hand to hold the base of his penis steady or to fondle the scrotum, take his shaft into your other hand, wrapping your fingers around it and warming it up with long strokes.

4. After you've established a rhythm with this motion and both of you are feeling more comfortable and relaxed, hold the penis with both hands so that your thumbs meet in front on the underside. Rub up and down very slowly, slowing even more when you get close to the top, just under the coronal ridge. The underside of the penis is more sensitive than the top side.

5. Consider this the foreplay of the hand job, leisurely taking your time moving up and down the shaft while teasing the corona every time you reach the top, running your thumb tips across it with firm pressure.

6. Eventually, you should wrap your middle finger around the area below the groove of his glans. (If he's uncircumcised, avoid rubbing his glans and be sure to pull his foreskin back as far as it will go.)

7. Make a motion as though twisting off a bottle cap; then grip the whole shaft with your hand and make a sweep down to the root.

8. Repeat. This action will stimulate the frenulum.

9. Check in with your partner to see if he's doing okay and if he wants you to move on. He is likely to be indifferent, but this is not to be taken as an insult. He's simply in heaven, and the utopia you're proposing doesn't look too different, but he's always willing to try another ethereal space.

10. Change up the twisting motion so that as you turn your wrist and open your hand, the flattest part of your palm rests on the head every time you stroke upward. Caress the glans with the center of your palm every time you move upward with this back-and-forth motion.

11. Just when it seems that he's on the brink of climax, move back to the frenulum. Using light brushing strokes or little circles, gradually increase your pressure on this spot as his excitement mounts.

12. Finish the job by going back to long, firm strokes up and down the shaft with one hand while using the fingers of your other hand to run circles around his corona. This will require the same kind of concentration as rubbing your stomach and patting your head at the same time, but the results will be well worth the effort.

Sexual-Health Considerations During Manual Stimulation

In order to protect yourself from sexually transmitted infections (STIs) when stimulating his penis or other parts of his genitals, consider wearing a latex glove to reduce the risk of transmission. Although manual stimulation is considered a low-risk sexual behavior for infections like HIV, there is a chance of transmission if semen comes in contact with any cuts or sores on the hands.

❦ TIPS FOR GREAT HAND JOBS ❧

Breath check.

This is not the type of breath check you usually worry about. Make sure your partner is breathing fully and deeply. Encourage him to do so if he isn't already, as this will make his orgasm even more incredible, spreading sensations throughout his body.

Vary your hand movement.

If you plan to manipulate the penis for a while, have your hands take turns with what they're doing so you don't get tired. Know that no matter what, it's the rhythmic motion of your stimulation, applied with just the right amount of pressure, that gets him off more than anything.

Hello, neighbor!

Get the testicles in on the action. With a lubricated or oiled hand, rub his perineum or anus. Tickle or cup and massage his testicles. Gently tug on the hairs covering his testicles. Lightly scratch his scrotum with your fingernails.

Don't ignore his other hot spots.

Tease his nipples or other favorite erogenous zones. Massage his chest or legs. Stimulate his anal area with your fingers or a sex toy.

Turn your hand into its own sex toy.

Wrap your thumb and index finger either around the base of the penis or, if you have big enough hands, the balls and shaft. Contracting them, with however much pressure your lover can handle, turns your hand into a live cock ring!

Double the fun.

If you get tired at any point or start wondering if there's something he wishes you were doing, have him show you what he likes. One trick: If you're tired or want to further excite him, start playing with yourself while you get him off.

Experiment with the penis's different hot spots.

Some of his hot spots may be more responsive than others to different kinds of touch. Take the time to squeeze, pinch, nibble, and tease any or all of them at different points in his sexual-response cycle.

Get your own hot spots involved.

Caress his penis between your breasts, running your palm up and down his penis in a massaging motion.

The frenulum is an area of the penis that can be pierced in order to provide sexual pleasure to both partners.

❧ EXERCISE 5.2: *Total-Penis Stimulation*

1. Using two fingers, press into his perineum. Gripping the penis with the other hand, caress the glans for about ten seconds before giving the shaft one quick up-and-down stroke.

2. Repeat, only this time give the penis two quick up-and-down strokes. Repeat, giving three quick strokes. Continue this process until he reaches climax.

3. If you don't want for him to climax quickly, change the type of stimulation and "milk" him. Alternating hands, start at the base of the penis and work your way up to the tip, as though "milking" his shaft.

4. Gradually increase your speed.

❧ EXERCISE 5.3: *Doggie-Style Hand Job*

1. Get into the rear-entry position, but without penetration.

2. The top partner (the one in back) is to reach around to stimulate the other partners' penis in any way they desire.

3. Mimicking thrusting, pay attention to specifically bumping up against the bottom partner's testicles as you continue to get him off.

This position allows the bottom partner to feel his partner's chest pressing into his back. He can masturbate himself at the same time if his partner wants to get busy with other hot spots.

Oral Action for Penis Pleasure

Stimulating the penis with the mouth creates absolute erotic electricity, charging him and sedating him at the same time. It's the ultimate form of stimulation. There are several positions through which you can provide oral action:

❋ The man can sit up, with his partner lying on their side while fellating (giving oral sex).

❋ He can lie down, with knees bent and pelvis propped on a pillow, while his partner lies between his legs on their stomach or sits or lies on top of him, feet pointing toward his face (this gives him a brilliant view of his lover's groin, turning him on even more).

❋ He can be in a "crab" position (i.e., leaning back with his weight on his hands and feet and his buttocks 8–12 inches in the air, with the giver sitting under him on their buttocks with their face buried in his crotch.

❋ The man can straddle the giver's chest, facing either way.

❋ He can be on all fours, with the giver lying under him.

Sexual-Health Considerations During Oral Stimulation

Several sexually transmitted infections (STIs) can be spread during unprotected oral sex, primarily herpes, genital warts, chlamydia, syphilis, gonorrhea, and HIV. Fellatio (oral sex performed on a man) is considered a high-risk sexual behavior for HIV transmission. To protect yourself, observe the following precautions:

⊙ *Don't brush or floss your teeth for at least two hours before giving head. Performing basic dental hygiene can create cuts or sores in your mouth, raising the risk of contracting an STI. Using a mild mouthwash can help you if you're worried about bad breath.*

⊙ *Use a latex condom over the penis. This barrier method helps to reduce the risk of transmission. If you're allergic to latex, polyurethane condoms are also available, though they're less effective since their breakage rate is almost four times that of latex (mostly because of reduced elasticity).*

◖ EXERCISE 5.4: *Oral Action Worthy of "Ohhhs"*

1. Covering your teeth with your lips, take his penis into your mouth and move your mouth up and down the shaft, being careful not to graze the penis with your teeth.

2. Once both of you are feeling warmed up, and he's nice and hard, explore the hot spots on his penis, starting with the glans. Move your tongue in a circular motion around the head of the penis.

3. Taking your time, flick your tongue along the shaft.

4. Eventually, move to flick your tongue horizontally across the corona only.

5. Give the corona relief on occasion by licking and sucking the frenulum.

6. When it seems that his hot spots have received all the stimulation they can take (and if he hasn't come yet), switch to licking the shaft in an up-and-down motion using long strokes.

7. Look for a blood vessel–like seam on the underside of his penis—his **R-spot** (raphe). Give it a long, firm lick, starting beneath his scrotum and moving to the tip of the shaft.

8. In preparation for the grand finale, move back to the corona and feast on it—kissing and nibbling it before hardening your tongue into a point and flicking across it.

9. Flatten your tongue and massage this spot using circular motions, first moving clockwise and then counterclockwise.

10. Finish by taking the head into your mouth, sucking it gently, and running your tongue back and forth along the coronal ridge once more.

11. Tighten your lips as you move up and down his shaft.

12. Take his penis deeper and deeper into your mouth, increasing your speed of oral thrusting. His Mount St. Helen's will soon erupt.

❧ TIPS FOR GREAT BLOW JOBS ☙

Build your speed.
Whatever your sucking rhythm and motion, begin gently at first and then gradually increase your speed

Keep your throat muscles relaxed.
This will help to prevent you from choking on his prized possession. Be sure to breathe through your nose, which should also help you to avoid gagging.

Give yourself a break if you need to.

You can do this by slapping his erection against your lips and tongue, humming for low-maintenance stimulation, or arousing his penis with other enhancements, like a sex toy, warming lubricant, or locks of your hair.

Keep it tasty.

Try a mint or flavored lube. They not only offer a kick for your taste buds, but they also give him a different kind of stimulation.

Titty fuck.

If you can, squeeze your breasts around the shaft of his penis as he thrusts. You can lick the head of the penis as it emerges from your breasts, and you can simultaneously stroke your own nipples.

What are your hands doing?

Don't let either or both hands get lazy. Keep them busy by loosely encircling one around the base of his penis and moving your hand and mouth rhythmically up and down the shaft. You can use the other one to massage his scrotum or to stimulate other erogenous hot spots, like the back of his knees or nipples.

Acupressure Points

There are a number of acupressure points that can be stimulated while a man is lost in penile pleasures. We have already hit on the Rushing Door and Mansion Cottage points (see Figure 5.2 on page 73).

◊ EXERCISE 5.5: *Powerful Points*

Stimulation of the St. 30 acupressure points, located just beside his penis at the tip of each pubic bone (see Figure 5.3 on the next page), further increases sensitivity in his genitals and heightens his sexual pleasure. These points can be stimulated using the base of your thumb during oral sex, or they can be kissed and sucked during manual stimulation.

◊ EXERCISE 5.6: *Times Two Doubles the Fun*

Two other acupressure points you can stimulate during oral or manual sex are the Crooked Bone point, in the center of the top edge of the pubic bone, and the Transverse Bone point, located on the upper border of the pubic bone, half a finger-width from the midline on either side (see Figure

5.3). As he lies on his back, kneel between his legs and place your fingers or mouth on these points. Alternatively, lie down on his entire body, gradually thrusting your pelvis toward his to stimulate these points.

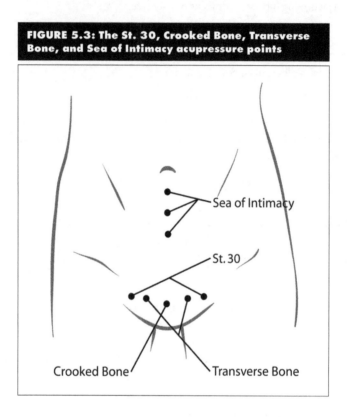

FIGURE 5.3: The St. 30, Crooked Bone, Transverse Bone, and Sea of Intimacy acupressure points

❧ EXERCISE 5.7: *Rockin' His World*

Activating his Sea of Intimacy acupressure points is one more option (see Figure 5.3). Located two, three, four, five, and six finger-widths below the navel, his Sea of Intimacy points can be stimulated by placing the heels of both hands over his pubic bone and gradually putting some of your weight onto his lower abdominal area while pressing into these points. This will heighten his sexual pleasure, unlock tension that can block sexual energy from flowing into his genitals during lovemaking, and strengthen his reproductive system. Try to breathe deeply together as you're doing this.

Yoga Poses for Penile Stimulation

◀ POSE 5.1: *Penile Stimulation and Heart Opener*

His position: Get into Camel Pose (Ustrasana) by getting onto your knees, which are spaced six to eight inches apart. Inhale and lift your torso as you lean back. Allow your head to drop as your hips press forward, slowly placing your right hand on your right heel and your left hand on your left heel. Press your hips into your partner's lower back and buttocks.

His partner's position: Get into Plow Pose (Halasana) by lying on your back, arms relaxed at your sides, legs straight. As you exhale, use your abdominals to bring your legs up and over your head, toes possibly touching the floor.

Hold for up to one minute.

YOGA POSE 5.1: Penile stimulation and heart opener

Results: This position will boost his sex drive, open his heart chakra, and allow him to channel energy into his partner's root chakra. It also provides penile stimulation.

◀ POSE 5.2: *Pelvic Stimulation*

Both partners' positions: Stand and face each other, bodies pressed against one another. Holding each other by clasping your hands around your partner's lower back, arch your upper bodies backward, keeping your feet well grounded to the floor.

Hold for up to two minutes.

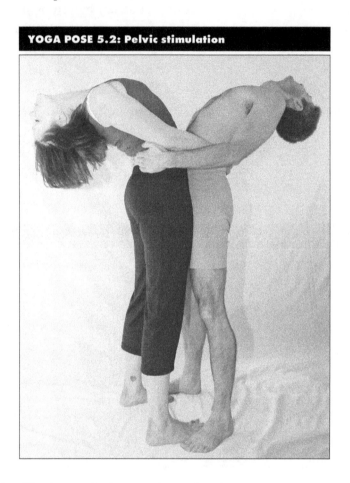

YOGA POSE 5.2: Pelvic stimulation

Results: This opens the heart and sacral chakras, improves circulation in the sexual organs of female partners, increases emotional well-being, and provides stimulation against both partner's pelvises, especially his penis.

Whether you're the giver or receiver, stimulating the penis is among the most gratifying experiences two lovers can share. To avoid getting into a monotonous routine, try trimming his pubic hair for different sensations, orally stimulating his penis through his boxers or G-string, making his penis more edible by adding whipped cream and chocolate sauce, or rubbing his penis with silk scarves. His penis will undoubtedly rise to the occasion. Also, check out the sex toys in Chapter 13 and consider how any of them may be able to provide his hot spots the ultimate in pleasure.

His Geyser-Producing G-Spot

When a man is sexually aroused, his **prostate** begins to swell with fluid, sending increasingly pleasurable sensations throughout his groin as he approaches climax. About the size of a chestnut, this little wonder surrounds the urethra, lying just under the bladder and behind the pubic bone directly above the perineum (see Figure 6.1). Also known as the **male G-spot**, the prostate is a firm gland composed of tiny blood vessels, plus muscle, glandular, and connective tissues that forcefully secrete some of the milky fluid that makes up semen. This fluid protects sperm by increasing the pH of their environment (making the vagina friendlier for fertilization), and it facilitates their movement after ejaculation. The prostate's nerve plexus is seen as contributing to a male's sexual emotional center in tantric practice.

Why Is the Prostate
One of the Hottest Spots?

The prostate is worthy of this label for a couple of reasons. Referred to in tantra as the Sacred Gate, when stimulated, this hot spot is a major moan zone, producing enhanced genital sensations and an intense, powerful, throbbing orgasm—or orgasms. Such unusual, amazingly pleasurable

FIGURE 6.1: The internal male genitalia

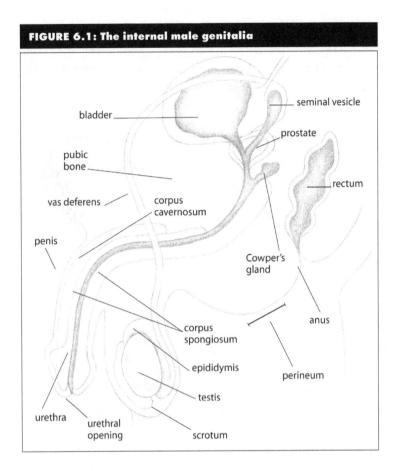

bladder

seminal vesicle

prostate

pubic bone

rectum

vas deferens

corpus cavernosum

penis

Cowper's gland

corpus spongiosum

anus

epididymis

perineum

testis

urethra

urethral opening

scrotum

sensations can occur with or without an erection, with or without other stimulation, and with or without ejaculation, making the prostate's gifts even more jaw dropping, especially when compared to a merely penis-focused understanding of male sexual response. The prostate is also credited with helping men to maintain erection when stimulated, thereby extending lovemaking.

Second, the prostate is most effectively stimulated through the rectum, and anything involving anal play is usually regarded by society as taboo, if not downright wrong, and thus ultimately racier and more intriguing. Some people get a high from doing something many others frown upon. Half the thrill is actually doing what others consider deviant (despite the fact that many people engage in all sorts of anal play). Plus, because so many people have issues with anal stimulation, successfully unearthing this buried treasure can make you feel like a sexual millionaire. You've reached a status many will never know, joining a members-only sex club of sorts where only the daring and adventurous share its secrets and rewards.

Prostate Myths and Misconceptions

Myth: Men are not blessed with the same hot spots women are, such as the clitoris and G-spot.

Your response to prostate stimulation depends on your particular physiology—you may enjoy your prostate as immensely as a woman does her clit or G-spot. Some men experience massive orgasm(s) when their prostate is stimulated, while others simply enjoy a great deal of pleasure. Some men don't enjoy prostate stimulation at all, others could take it or leave it, and still others thinks it's to die for. Given its often-rave reviews, it's certainly worth experimenting with, *non?*

Myth: Prostate stimulation is a pleasure only reserved for gay males.

Men of all sexual orientations enjoy prostate pleasure, but homophobia often fosters ideas indicating otherwise. It's a shame that some men get hung up on worries that they'll "turn" gay or bisexual if they engage in any sort of prostate or anal play. Engaging in a particular sex act does not necessarily mean that a person is of a certain sexual orientation. Every man has a G-spot and every man has the potential to enjoy it, regardless of whom or what turns him on.

Prostate-Triggered Orgasm

A man's orgasm always begins at his prostate, moving into the penis and testicles, possibly becoming a total-body experience. Most effectively induced by stimulating the prostate via the rectum, a **prostate-triggered orgasm** is a deeper, implosive, more full-bodied, longer-lasting orgasm, with ejaculation coming in spurts instead of in a steady stream. Many men claim that it is the best orgasm of their lives, having never experienced anything like it before.

A headline-worthy claim of prostate-stimulation feats is that this hot spot is one of the most effective ways for a man to experience multiple orgasms, including "dry" (without ejaculation) orgasms. Like women who experience a blended orgasm from simultaneous G-spot and clitoral stimulation, men can experience their own **"blended" orgasm** if their prostate and penis are stimulated at the same time, further increasing their chances of having multiple Os.

Rules for Prostate Play

* Make sure he's becoming aroused or is fully aroused before stimulating the prostate. If this isn't the case, prostate play can be painful and uncomfortable.

* Confirm that there's mutual interest and consent. Both partners need to be willing to explore and must feel comfortable and relaxed.

* Be open-minded. Let go of expectations. You need to trust each other, and the receiver needs to feel comfortable with not being in control, a position many men aren't used to during sex.

* Empty your bladder beforehand; this will help you avoid thinking you need to pee, a feeling you're likely to have when your prostate is first stimulated.

* Make sure that your nails are trimmed, especially if you're not using gloves.

* Use lots of lube. The brands Probe, Anal Eze, or Wet are often used for anal sex play.

* Communicate. You need to find out what does and doesn't feel good. You need to express how you're feeling and what you need more or less of.

* Take your time stimulating his G-spot. Also, be prepared to do so on multiple occasions if this is an activity you really want to incorporate into your sex life. This type of sexual stimulation takes time and practice. You'll see more and better results with practice. Plus, with experience, you'll become more at ease, making the whole process sexier and simply exquisite.

✳ Explore on your own. By self-pleasuring, you can become more comfortable with your anal area and more used to having it stimulated, which will help immensely when you're with a partner.

Cleanliness is often a concern when it comes to fooling around with the exit-only area. If you or your partner has issues with cleanliness, consider the following tactics to make both of you more comfortable during prostate pleasuring:

- *Take a shower before and after prostate play.*
- *Wear gloves, rolling them off from the wrist when you're done.*
- *Use an anal douche kit ahead of time.*
- *Have towels, handiwipes, hand sanitizer, and a garbage bag readily available in case they're needed.*
- *Wash your hands right after sex play.*

Consider using a sex toy, preferably one that is covered with a condom, to deal with any cleanliness issues, at least until you're more comfortable with prostate play. Acrylic anal toys that have a wide safety base are recommended for stimulating the anus.

Finger Action for Prostate Pleasure

There are a number of positions a man can utilize to have his prostate stimulated. He can

✳ lie down on his back with his knees bent and feet flat on the floor or bed, or with his knees drawn up to his chest

✳ kneel

✳ sit, leaning back against a support or wall

✳ squat

✳ get on his hands and knees

✳ lie on his side

✳ lie on his stomach (which offers the most direct way to stimulate the prostate)

Placing a pillow or prop under his buttocks will make some positions easier.

❦ EXERCISE 6.1: *Pleasuring the Prostate*

To locate and stimulate the prostate gland, perform the following exercise:

1. Sit between your partner's legs, and once he's sexually aroused, slowly insert the tip of your well-lubricated index finger into his anus.

2. Check in with your partner to see how he's doing. If he's comfortable, continue to insert your finger up to the second knuckle.

3. About two or three inches inside the rectum, along the front rectal wall (the side toward the stomach), you'll be able to feel the prostate through the wall. It will feel like a walnut or dome.

4. If he's not fully relaxed, simply hold the area by pressing your finger firmly against the prostate for ten to thirty seconds. You can also slowly move your fingers in and out of the anus in a light thrusting motion.

5. Once both of you are feeling more comfortable, press gently against the prostate, curling your finger upward to execute a firm "come-hither" motion. (Your entire finger will need to be in the anus. It may be easier to use your middle finger.)

6. Your fingertip will be tapping or rubbing against his prostate, so ask your partner if he would like for your touch to be a little more firm and if he prefers one motion more than the other.

7. Gently stroke the gland in a downward direction, massaging it. Check in with your partner to find out what he would like for you to do or continue doing to gradually bring him to one of the best orgasms of his whole life!

If he loses his erection at any point, don't take this as a sign that there's necessarily something wrong. He may just be uncomfortable and need to relax more fully. Also, with all of his attention on his prostate and anus, he is not going to be focusing on his penis, which is another reason it may go slack. He may still be having a ball, so make sure to ask him how he's doing and avoid making a big deal over whether or not he has an erection, or how strong or weak it is.

❧ TIPS ☙

Combine acts.
At the same time that you're pleasuring his prostate, stimulate his penis manually by massaging it or orally by simply sucking on it like a lollipop; this will double the incredible sensations he's experiencing.

Spice up the finger action.
Once you're comfortable and more experienced with his responses and preferences, slowly slide your fingers rhythmically from side to side across his G-spot. Switch to firmly rocking your finger(s) from side to side across this erogenous zone.

Thrust.
Work your finger, or fingers, in and out of the anus, exerting pressure upward to stimulate his G-spot every time you go deep.

Cuddle the prostate.
Push his penis toward his lower abs. This causes the roots of the corpus cavernosa to internally massage his prostate.

Sexual Health Considerations

Sexually transmitted infections (STIs), including hepatitis B and HIV, can be spread when stimulating the prostate via the anal canal, so consider wearing a latex glove to reduce the risk of transmission, especially if you have any cuts or sores on your hands. Furthermore, after anal play do not insert a finger or a sex toy into a woman's vagina or a partner's anus without washing it first, as this can cause infection.

Perineum

The perineum, or **P-spot**, the acupressure point known as Inner Meeting or Hui-Yin, meaning the Gate of Life and Death, is the patch of skin, rich in nerve endings, that lies between a man's testicles and anus (see Figure

6.1 on page 85). (In a woman, the perineum lies between the vaginal opening and the anus.) In the male, stimulating this muscular band of flesh can result in both prostate and penile stimulation. It is further renowned for its role in delaying ejaculation when pressed, especially when long, firm pressure is applied at the same time that a man takes slow, deep breaths. For couples who would like to stimulate the prostate but have issues with anal play, try pressing against his perineum with the ball of your thumb.

Yet another reason why the perineum is a well-appreciated hot spot is because of its role in moving the body's energy. Reflexology holds that there are two channels for circulating chi, the energy that helps to remove blockages in the meridians, activating more energy and revitalizing the body. The first channel, known as the Conception or Functional meridian, begins in the perineum, at the base of the body's trunk, in both males and females. It travels along the front of the body, going past the genitals, stomach, heart, and throat to end at the tip of the tongue. The second channel, called the Governor meridian, begins in the same location and travels along the back of the body, into the tailbone, up through the spine, and into the brain. From there it loops back down through the roof of the mouth. Stimulating the perineum is said to help facilitate this circulation of energy.

Finger and Oral Action for Perineal Pleasuring

When you press the perineum, you'll feel the bone close to the scrotum and a spongy area closer to the anus. To find the prostate gland, which sits directly above the perineum, you'll need to feel for a slight indentation or ropy cord. Once found, you can indirectly stimulate the prostate, as well as the base of the penis, by using one long, firm push or several rhythmic pushes. You can also caress it, tap it, massage it, tongue it, stroke it with your fingertips, use your fingers to vibrate against it, or use an actual vibrator or other sex toy on it. Pushing against it with your palm or the second knuckle of your middle finger, possibly vibrating it, is especially effective as well. Regardless of what you do, it's important to press softly at first and to vary the direction and amount of pressure every now and then. Try going in clockwise circles, then switching to counterclockwise circles. Massage up and down, then from side to side, then diagonally. No matter what your style, try to stimulate the anal opening or his penis, possible cupping his scrotum at times, as you tease the perineum. Other hot spots must not be ignored!

⁌ EXERCISE 6.2: *The Perineal Pause*

1. Run your first three fingers down the crevice of his buttocks, stopping at his perineum.

2. Gently press his P-spot for a full second.

3. Sweep your fingers back up the crevice.

4. Make sure he's breathing fully throughout the exercise. Ask him if he would like more pressure or if you need to adjust the placing of your pressure.

5. Repeat steps 1–3, this time firmly applying pressure with your fingers for two full seconds.

6. Continue this press-and-release move several times, adding a second each time.

For additional stimulation, use the palm of your hand to roll his penis against his belly from side to side, gradually increasing your speed. Activating his Sea of Intimacy points (see Figure 5.3 on page 80) at the same time you press on the Inner Meeting point (the P-spot; see Figure 6.1 on page 85) is another option. Encourage him to move his pelvis into your hands as you hold these points for a couple of minutes.

A Workout Like No Other:
Strengthening the PC Muscle

The perineum is intimately involved in better sex, especially in the toning of the **pubococcygeus muscle (PC muscle)**, a term used for the group of pelvic-floor muscles that are attached to the pelvic bone and that serve to hold in the pelvic organs. Referred to as the "chi muscle" in sexual reflexology, the PC muscle runs from the pubic bone to the tailbone, encircling the base of the penis and the rectum, naturally contracting when a man climaxes. This muscle group is such a big deal because the **pudendal nerve** runs through it and triggers most of the muscular reactions during arousal and stimulation, sending and receiving signals to and from the brain.

As described in Chia and Abrams' *The Multi-Orgasmic Man,* Eastern approaches to sex are adamant about the need to increase one's PC-muscle strength for better sex and overall health. Strengthening the PC muscle can help a man become multiorgasmic, have better erections, delay and control orgasms, have a shorter refractory period, be more energetic, increase orgasmic intensity, and keep the prostate healthy. When a man is able to regulate his climactic contractions, making them slower, he is able to expand his orgasm and pump sexual energy throughout the path of his chakras.

To find your PC muscle, feel just behind your testicles and in front of your anus. One way to identify the muscle is to stop your urine flow in midstream by contracting your pelvic-floor muscles. You may experience a slight stinging sensation when you do this. Another way to find this muscle is by pushing down with your pelvic area as though you were having a bowel movement. By repeating either action a few times, you will become familiar with the feel of contracting the correct group of muscles. Note: Do not contract your abdominal, thigh, or buttocks muscles while performing the following exercises.

❧ EXERCISE 6.3: *Pump This*

To strengthen your PC muscle, perform the following routine:

1. Slowly hold and release your PC muscle ten to thirty times at the same rate at which you breathe (contract the muscle as you inhale and release as you exhale). Repeat twice a day or three times in one set, with thirty-second breaks between sets, focusing on your prostate, perineum, and anus. Make sure that you're breathing deeply and fully with each squeeze.

2. As you gain strength, gradually increase the number of repetitions to seventy-five, twice a day. Up to three hundred reps per day is recommended for those who have developed great control over this muscle.

As you become more advanced in your practice, you can hold the contraction for a count of three instead of releasing it immediately. Relax and repeat as many times as you are able, working up to about fifty of these longer contractions. Another version involves inhaling and doing ten mini-contractions before exhaling and relaxing. This can be repeated as many times as you are able to, and you can work your way up to doing fifty sets per day.

His Don't-Forget-to-
Detonate Spot

The **testicles**, also known as the **testes**, or **gonads**, are a pair of oval glands that produce sperm and sex hormones, primarily testosterone. These gems are housed in and protected by the **scrotum**, the dark, thin-skinned pouch based below the root of the penis that contains numerous fatty glands and is covered with hair (See Figure 5.1 on page 64).

Testicles vary in size and shape from man to man, with the left testicle usually hanging lower than the right one and with one usually being larger than the other. Some are big and loose in appearance, while others are small and tight. To regulate temperature for prime sperm manufacturing, the scrotum contracts muscles that bring the testes closer to the body when cold or relaxes muscles to lower the testes away from the body when too warm. During sexual excitement the testes become engorged with blood, growing up to 50 percent larger than they are in an unaroused state.

Testicular Myths and Misconceptions

Myth: The scrotal sac isn't very sensitive—men don't get a lot of pleasure from its stimulation.

95

The scrotal sac is very sensitive in that it's full of nerve endings. Some men love to have it stimulated and others do not. Furthermore, the **R-spot** of the scrotum, the male's **raphe**, provides pleasurable sensations if given proper attention. A visible line along the center and underside of the scrotum, the scrotal raphe can be stimulated by gently running your fingertips along it.

Myth: All men like to have their scrotum stimulated the same way.
Scrotal sensitivity, reactivity, and preferences vary from male to male. What turns one guy on might be a total turn-off to the next. When playing with his testicles, be sure to ask what feels good, what kinds of sensations he likes (or doesn't), and if he wants more or less stimulation. Sometimes a man won't express himself, feeling that he either has to be stoic during sexual pleasuring or must put up with discomfort and pain "like a man."

Rules for Testicular Play

❈ Make sure your nails are trimmed and that you don't have any hangnails. Testicular tissue is very delicate and sensitive.

❈ Be gentle as you start to toy with the testicles. The scrotum is no punching bag.

❈ Unless a man likes it, avoid pinching, squeezing, biting, or clawing too hard.

Hand Action for Testicular Pleasure

Caressing, scratching, pulling, rubbing, and squeezing the scrotal sac will result in *ooh-là-là* sensations for many men, as long as these actions are done with tender, loving care. Some men can handle more stimulation than others. Be sure to check in with a man about his arousal level to see how efforts are paying off, as he may be too far gone in ecstasy to be fully present and communicative or may be wincing from pain to the point where he's speechless. It's important to make sure that you're not overstimulating this area, which can make things simply uncomfortable and unpleasant. There's one nonverbal, however, that will prove your efforts are a success: As a male becomes more and more excited, his scrotum tightens and contracts.

For even more titillating action, consider pleasuring the three sensitive and arousing acupressure points that exist inside the upper thigh, the Inner Thigh points, which are located close to the crease that joins the thigh with the trunk of the body (see Figure 7.1). These points are stimulated naturally during many intercourse positions; during other types of sex play, try to hold and press them for greater sexual fulfillment. Doing this increases circulation to his reproductive organs, heightening sensitivity in his genitals and breathing even more life into the scrotum.

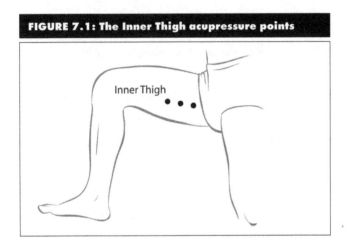

FIGURE 7.1: The Inner Thigh acupressure points

Inner Thigh

Other acupressure points that can be held with your fingertips while orally stimulating the testicles are the Rushing Door and Mansion Cottage points, located in the center of the leg crease at the top of the thigh (see Figure 5.2 on page 73). Holding them for one minute will result in pulsations between these points and the genitals. Yet another acupressure point to work while titillating the scrotal sac is his perineum.

◈ EXERCISE 7.1: *Scrotal Focus*

1. Straddle your partner, facing his feet, your weight on your knees. He is lying with his knees bent, feet flat on the floor.

2. Slowly, lightly, touch the Inner Thigh pressure points for a couple of minutes, working your way up the crease toward his hip.

3. Using the other hand, luxuriously massage his testicles.

4. Intermittently, press on his perineum.

A variation on this exercise involves you lying on his stomach and gently licking and kissing these acupressure points, especially as a prelude to oral sex.

Another activity for the "dragon pearls" that a man can do on his own is known as testicle breathing. As explained in Chia and Wei's *Sexual Reflexology,* this exercise, recommended by Taoists, transforms his raw sexual energy into a higher energy, nourishing the spine, nervous system, brain, and other organs.

⬗ EXERCISE 7.2: *Taoist Testicle Breathing*

1. Sitting and remaining relaxed, massage your testicles for a few minutes.

2. Slightly contract your left testicle, mentally drawing its energy up through your tailbone, sacrum, and spine, eventually to your brain.

3. As you return this energy to your scrotum, place your tongue against the roof of your mouth.

4. Repeat using your right testicle.

With practice and mindfulness, you'll eventually feel energy rising up from your testicle.

⬗ TIPS ⬖

Use lube.
The scrotal sac is already a smooth area, but using lube will help things be silky smooth, making the experience all the better.

Tickle time.
Stroke the hair around his scrotum and anus, at first barely touching the skin.

"Hand" him different sensations.
Try wearing different types of gloves to provide a variety of sensations. From time to time, experiment with satin gloves, leather gloves, gloves for body washing, etc.

Curl up.

Having him bring his thighs up toward his chest will allow either partner to feel the testicles more easily and will afford more access to the perineum and anus for stimulation of those regions.

Heat things up.

Take his balls into your mouth and simply let him relish the heat and moisture of your tongue. To make him feel weak in the knees, breathe in through your nose and then force the hot air out from your lungs, the same way you would when making the sound "huh."

Oral Action for Testicular Pleasure

If you want to add oral exploits to the equation, continue to handle the scrotum delicately, being careful not to scrape it with your teeth (covering them with your lips can help). Try humming for added sensation. Applying a drop of lubricant and then lightly wrapping the scrotal sac in plastic wrap will further enhance your vocal vibrations. Also, the increase in temperature from the testicles being wrapped will cause his blood vessels to dilate, resulting in more blood flow to the penis and a stronger erection.

Your efforts may be enhanced if he gets on all fours above you, with your hands free to caress other parts of his body, like his buttocks, perineum, penis, or treasure trail (the line of hair running from his navel to his pubic area). This position can also double the fun by allowing you to incorporate "69" sex play, which involves both partners performing oral sex on each other at the same time.

"69"

A great form of foreplay or the main show, 69 allows you to enjoy sexual stimulation while you simultaneously stimulate your partner. Think of it as total-body sex. In experimenting with 69, take turns being on the top and on the bottom. This sexual feat can also be attempted with both partners lying side-by-side while facing opposite directions, with each partner's upper leg bent, foot on the floor or bed, in order to better expose the genitals.

Sixty-nine is great for variety, the thrill of mutual stimulation, and the eroticism of sex galore, but it is not the most effective position for getting off (which isn't to say it doesn't happen!). It can be quite difficult to both give and receive, and you may struggle over whose pleasure to concentrate on more. If it gets to be too complicated and frustrating, take turns feasting on each other—and turn to your partner's testicles if you're the one receiving more attention. Giving the testicles some warm, wet licks and sucks is one way to keep 69 alive while not getting carried away (or overworked) with the efforts needed for penile oral stimulation.

◀ EXERCISE 7.3: *The Pull with Punch*

The cremaster muscle, which lines the inside of the scrotum, extends into the groin, controlling testicular contractions when a male is cold, hot, or turned on. As a man gets closer to orgasm, this muscle contracts, causing the testicles to recede. The next time you're going down on him, cup his scrotal sac with one hand and gently pull it away from his body as he's about to reach climax. This will cause the cremaster muscle to delay ejaculation, prolonging his pleasure. As you get to know his response and comfort level, you may be able to pull slightly harder (be sure to ask him first). You can also use both hands to delicately "milk" his testicles, like you would a cow, matching the rhythm of the up-and-down motion of your oral thrusting.

Yoga Poses for Testicular Stimulation

◀ POSE 7.1: *Perineal and Scrotal Stimulation*

His position: Bringing the left leg up toward your lover's shoulder, make a split over their pelvis. Leaning forward, grab your left big toe with the first two fingers of your left hand (see picture on facing page).

His partner's position: Lying on your back, pull your left leg up for Reclined Big Toe Pose (Supta Padangusthasana), holding your calf with both hands. While exhaling, hold your left big toe with the first two fingers of your left hand. Lower this leg toward your left shoulder.

Hold for two minutes. This position can also be performed using the opposite leg.

YOGA POSE 7.1: Perineal and scrotal stimulation

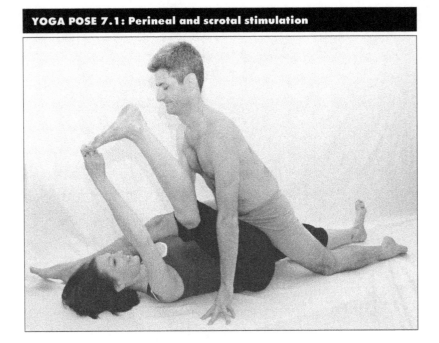

Results: This pose provides hot pelvis-on-pelvis stimulation, especially for the perineal and scrotal areas.

◖ POSE 7.2: *Scrotal and Root Chakra Stimulation*

His position: Lying on your back, with both knees bent into your chest, rest your head on the floor (see picture on page 102).

His partner's position: Straddling his legs, squat so that your buttocks rest on his. Clasping his hands may help your balance.

Hold this position for up to three minutes, maintaining eye contact and breathing in unison.

Results: The root chakra is filled with energy, which relaxes the entire area. Partners strengthen their bond as they merge through mutual eye gazes and breathing. His scrotum is stimulated.

Consider incorporating all of the spots we've covered into the sexual positions described in Chapter 14. Lovers often assume that: (A) a man is

YOGA POSE 7.2: Scrotal and root chakra stimulation

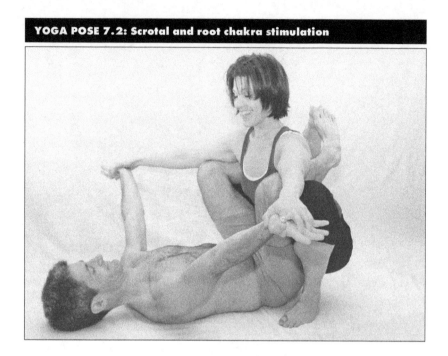

happy just to be having sex and (B) missionary or doggie style seems to suit him just fine, so why do anything else? It's just as fun for men as it is for women to switch things up, experiment with different types of pleasure, and pay extraordinary attention to his various erogenous areas, so go ahead and indulge him!

8

The Play-with-Me Spots

While not the most hyped-up hot spots, the erogenous zones we cover in the next five chapters are really where the action is and where one's full erotic potential lies. These are the areas that assist you in seduction, that help you to come alive during foreplay, and that make orgasms total-body experiences. Incorporating the breast, head, body, anal region, hands, and feet into your sex play can take your lovemaking to heights you've never known, with your only potential regret being, "Why didn't I think of this sooner?"

Called the "bells of love" by Chinese sexologists, **breasts** are secondary sex organs, packed with pleasure-receptive nerve endings that send sensations to the brain in the same way the genitals do. In women, each breast is composed of fatty and fibrous tissues that surround fifteen to twenty clusters of mammary glands. The mammary glands, each of which has a separate opening to the nipple, are capable of producing milk.

The **nipples** of both sexes are surrounded by the areola and consist of smooth muscle fibers that cause them to become erect; for example, when cold or aroused. During sexual stimulation, the nipples fill with blood, becoming more sensitive to touch in some individuals. Depending on the person's skin tone, the areola can be any shade of brown, black, or pink; it may protrude, be flat, or be inverted in shape. With sexual excitement, the areolas darken and may become more erect, firm, or prominent.

Besides their visual appeal, the breasts are an active center of sexual energy. Sexual reflexology claims that the muscles underlying the breast directly reflect the genitals. Furthermore, a tremendous amount of sexual energy is freed by moving energy in and around the breast area, since the stomach channel, a primary meridian, runs through the breast. All of these facts, along with the many love points located throughout the chest area, make the breasts a glorious, double-your-fun erogenous hot spot.

The nipples, specifically, hold love points called Center of the Breasts (see Figure 8.1), which arouse sexual energy. These can be stimulated by rolling the nipple between the thumb and index finger, applying pressure gradually as both lovers breathe deeply. The Heavenly Pond points, one thumb-width out from each nipple (see Figure 8.1), increase sexual intimacy and help to express love and affection when touched or held, especially while the nipple is sucked. One of a pair of love points also lies under each breast, beneath the breastbone. Any of these points can be lightly stroked or pressed with a palm or finger.

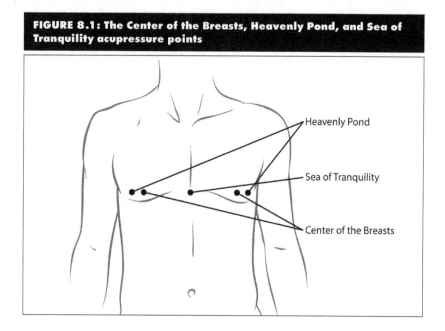

FIGURE 8.1: The Center of the Breasts, Heavenly Pond, and Sea of Tranquility acupressure points

In traditional Chinese medicine, massaging the breast is encouraged for the prevention of breast cancer and the promotion of better health. Doing so is said to stimulate the flow of blood and chi throughout the body. Massaging the breast particularly targets circulation in the lymphatic system, a network of vessels that purifies blood throughout the body, keeping it healthy.

Nipple-Induced Orgasm

Some women can reach orgasm through breast stimulation alone, especially nipple stimulation. Note that breast size bears no relation to breast and nipple sensitivity. Some women experience orgasm during breast-feeding, despite not being sexually aroused, due to the stimulation of the nipples and the release of oxytocin, a hormone that causes uterine contractions. This is a perfectly natural, normal response.

Involving the nipples in sex play is one way a person can have an entire-body orgasm. With one hand stimulating her clitoris or his penis and the other moving over the nipple, an individual can be brought to climax. The two different body parts, nipple and genitals, must be caressed with the same intensity, rhythm, and movements; for example, circular, up-down, or left-right. If you want sexual sensations to linger and to take your time working through the response cycle, back off from double stimulation. Take turns giving each spot a break, allowing your lover to feel the quivers of each locale's varying sensations. Stimulating your partner's ears and lips will expand the sensations even more.

Breast Myths and Misconceptions

Myth: Men aren't into nipple stimulation.

Many men have very sensitive nipples. Regardless of how sensitive they are, some men enjoy having them stimulated. Since the breasts are usually regarded as more erogenous in females, many men may be embarrassed to ask their partner to stimulate their nipples or may be shy about such sex play. Reassuring him that you think it's sexy to play with his nipples will help him to feel more confident about it.

Myth: All women's nipples are sensitive.

Not all women have sensitive nipples, leaving some to feel less sexual if they don't have the expected response to breast play. Even when a woman's nipple muscles contract during arousal, she may not have great sensitivity. Furthermore, since the entire breast is covered with rich nerve endings, she may find another area of the breast more sensitive than the nipple.

Myth: Bigger breasts make for more sensitive breasts.

All breasts, no matter what their size, have the same number of nerve endings. In fact, a woman with smaller breasts may experience more sensations during stimulation because her nerve endings are more condensed.

Rules for Breast and Nipple Pleasuring

* Don't twist. While many of us grew up hearing about the game Tune in Tokyo, in which a female's breasts are turned like radio knobs, in most cases this doesn't feel good.

* With both genders, start out gently. You need to warm up this sex organ as you would the others. Being too rough too quickly may cause pain and discomfort.

* Being vigorous is not always appropriate and can cause pain or numbness, especially for a woman around the time of her period, when her breasts are more tender.

* Communicate. There may be specific times when a person desires breast play. Some like it earlier in foreplay and others prefer a rougher sensation right at orgasm. See what works best for your partner.

Finger and Oral Action for Breast and Nipple Pleasure

For breast play, start out softly, unless you know that your partner prefers it rough. Beginning with the underside of the breast is an option, especially since this sensitive area is often ignored. Try kissing and touching the breasts, moving from the outside toward the nipple and lingering on the love points. Allow for some anticipation, using time as a tease before you reach the bull's-eye.

With your hand or fingers, massage the nipple in slow circles, gradually using firmer and firmer pressure. Wet your fingertips and squeeze the nipple between them. As the nipples harden, bring one to your mouth. Periodically, pull away to stimulate another hot spot, always bringing the focus back to the breasts. Every time you come back, vary the intensity of your tongue's pressure, perhaps using more pressure and faster and faster swipes. Become animalistic in your wanton desire to be completely engulfed in your lover's breasts.

Experiment with different sensations; some may get your partner off more than others. Try sucking, licking, touching, stroking, kissing, vibrating, slightly twisting, scratching, caressing, tweaking, pinching, clamping, tickling, teasing, nibbling, lightly biting.... Everybody is different, so make sure to check in with your lover to find out what feels good, what doesn't, if more pressure is needed, and if they want something else done.

Adjusting the temperature can stimulate the way any hot spot reacts to stimulation, but this is especially true of the nipples. Periodically, pull away and just graze the area with your hair or your lips, letting your hot breath linger on one nipple, then on the other. Blow on the nipple, making your breath either hot or cool. Drip warm wax (which you've tested beforehand) on the nipples. The heat and the hardening of the wax will have a double-whammy effect. On a hot day, lightly rub ice cubes on the chest to produce an instant nipple erection. The result: The nipples will tingle, harden, and send shivers throughout the whole body.

❦ TIPS ❧

Build anticipation.
Just like you would with below-the-belt hot spots, tease this area with light touches and intermittent attention, touching and caressing the areas around it, such as the collarbone, stomach, and armpits.

Lube it up.

Use lube at times, experimenting with different sensation-producing flavors; for example, cinnamon. This is especially superb for those times when your partner wants to squeeze the breasts together around your penis, turning them into a sexy toy for "titty fucking."

Play a numbers game.

Try practicing different tongue moves; for example, repeating the same number of strokes, tracing your path backward each time. Use the tip of the tongue to make little circles around the areola. Use the flat of the tongue to cover more surface area.

Make it the other kind of hand job.

Use different parts of your hand to stimulate the breast, from your fingertips to the palm. Even try the back of your hand to create a feeling of smoothness.

Nurse the breasts.

Create a slight suction with your mouth, building up this sensation if desired. The suction brings extra blood to the surface of the skin, making the nipple even more sensitive.

Try not always revealing the entire breast.

Your partner may want to leave their shirt or bra on during sex, so pull and knead the breasts under the garment or ask if your lover prefers the sensation of fabric against nipples. Any top or brassiere with a peekaboo effect is going to be extremely enticing for both partners.

Pay attention to the whole breast.

Don't ignore a person's breasts in favor of the nipples. The entire breast is responsive. Caress, knead, and gently squeeze the whole breast, perhaps massaging one breast as you give the other oral action.

Heart

The heart, home to the heart chakra in tantric practice, is strongly connected to your sexual center. In sexual reflexology, it is associated with the fire element. This energetic center of passion and affection is one hot spot. Opening the heart chakra is said to result in warmth, openness, relating well with others sexually, and the reciprocation of physical touch. If lovers are holding negative energy in this area, they need to unblock it to avoid negative emotions. Expressing what is in the heart frees this negative energy, turning it into something positive.

In acupressure, the heart point is known as the Sea of Tranquility. It is an emotional balancing point that opens and calms the heart's spirit. It lies in the center of the breastbone, four finger-widths up from the base of the bone (see Figure 8.1 on page 104). Stimulating it will help to relax a partner who is anxious, nervous, or tense, as well as increasing their inner joy and emotional intensity. You can do this by feeling for a dimple in the breastbone and then gently pressing into this point with your fingers for a couple of minutes, all while breathing in unison with your lover. You can also kiss and suck on this area as your lover arches their back for better stimulation, or you can give each other a full-body hug. Gazing into each other's eyes during the stimulation of this acupressure point will further intensify the experience, causing couples to feel even closer.

🍂 EXERCISE 8.1: *Holding Your Lover's Heart*

1. Place your right hand over your beloved's heart and have them do the same to you.

2. Place your left hand over your lover's right hand, pressing it into your heart. Have your lover do the same. The upper hand will transmit energy between the two of you.

3. Imagine that each of you is sending love energy from your own heart, down your right arm, and out of your hand into the other's heart.

4. Make sure to breathe deeply, move slowly, and allow yourself to feel the energy that's being passed.

5. Close your eyes and breathe together.

6. Complete this exercise with a big, long hug, placing one hand on your partner's breastbone and the other directly behind on the upper back.

Two variations: Each partner can place their right hand on the other's genitals (with one's own left hand over the partner's right hand) or in the middle of the other's back, behind the heart (with one's own left hand placed over one's own heart).

❦ EXERCISE 8.2: *Stimulating Your Lover's Heart*

1. Stand facing your partner, reaching your hands around their back and lightly rubbing the area between their shoulder blades to warm and stimulate it.

2. As you continue to massage, gradually move closer until your chests are pressed against one another's.

3. Slowly give a deeper massage while holding each other.

Result of either exercise: Energy will pass through your lover's heart.

Yoga Pose for Chest Stimulation

❦ POSE 8.1: *Sex Nerve Stretch*

One partner's position: Sit in your lover's lap in Cobbler's Pose (Baddha Konasana), where the soles of your feet are together, spine straight, knees resting on your partner's, while holding onto your partner's big toes. As you lean back, you can feel each other's heartbeats.

YOGA POSE 8.1: Sex nerve stretch

Other partner's position: Sit on the floor, wrapping your legs and arms around your partner, taking hold of their big toes while straightening your spine.

Hold for ten breaths, breathing air slowly into your pelvic floor.

Results: This pose will stretch the muscles needed for advanced sex positions and will open the root, sacral, and heart chakras. It stretches the "sex nerve" in the inner thigh as well as the channels that benefit the reproductive systems of both sexes, specifically the kidney, liver, and spleen meridians.

The Mind-Blowing Spots

Your head is covered with a plethora of hot spots, and it houses the most significant one of all. If a misconception exists about any of the erogenous zones discussed in this chapter, it's that their pleasure capacity is secondary—that they're not where all of the action ultimately happens, so they're less interesting. This notion couldn't be further from the truth. Not only do these body parts turn us on and heat things up, but making them the sole focus of sex play can result in climax. When coupled with erotic thoughts or fantasies, touching any one of these spots can trigger what's known as an **extragenital orgasm,** or **spontaneous orgasm,** an orgasm that is reached *without* genital contact.

When you stimulate any of these areas, give them as much attention as you would the genitals. Be open-minded to everything they have to offer—there really are no limits. Embracing them as hot spots will enable you to get off in ways you may have been unaware of, ways you've never imagined. As we'll discuss in more detail at the end of this chapter, your mindset during sex play is your most powerful tool in helping you attain peaks of sexual pleasure. If you allow your expectation to be "anything can happen," you may end up magnificently, erotically surprised.

The Scalp

Giving your partner a head massage is one of the most sensual, soothing ways to seduce, show your love to, or simply pamper your partner. Massaging the scalp helps lovers to relax because it releases oxytocin, a stress-response hormone that produces a state of calm, especially in women, and enhances sexual pleasure. A scalp massage is a lovely form of foreplay and a terrific way to unwind together, whether or not you're up for more heart-pumping intimacy later.

Playing with your partner's hair during a head massage can also be a very luscious activity. In Taoist medicine, an abundance of hair is considered a sign of strong sexuality and great sexual energy, especially in men, so think about this as you twirl, twist, and stroke your lover's sensuous strands. If your partner doesn't have any hair, then you have an even better opportunity to work the scalp, running your fingers over its smooth, softly textured skin.

As you perform the following massages, take your time. Stay relaxed and breathe deeply as you work the stress and toxins out of your love's skin and muscles. Imagine that you're the one receiving the massage so you can better gauge the pace and pressure to use. What would feel good to you? Where should you linger? What part needs revisiting? Don't be afraid to interrupt the massage to ask where more or less stimulation is needed. You may not always get a response, however, which is a pretty good sign that you're doing a fabulous job. Likewise, be aware of your partner's responses that indicate your efforts are paying off; for example, the body slumping, moans, and heavier breathing. Be sensitive to any tension points, giving them extra attention. Stay in the moment, enjoying the touch, the intimacy, and the bonding, and be mindful not to rush. Giving and receiving loving touch is one of life's greatest gifts.

There are fifteen acupoints on the head: three between the eyebrows and front hairline, and twelve between the front and back hairline.

The following head massage is most easily performed with the masseuse sitting behind the receiving partner. The importance of taking your time as you proceed step-by-step cannot be emphasized enough.

◈ EXERCISE 9.1: *A Head Massage to Die For*

1. Luxuriously run your fingers through your lover's hair.

2. Carefully grab and lightly pull fistfuls of hair near their scalp, which helps relieve any tension.

3. Scratch the scalp, being careful not to dig in too much. Use your nails to make long sweeping strokes over the curve of the head. If you don't have nails, use your fingertips to provide more of a kneading action.

4. Switch to a shorter scratch that mimics an attempt to pick up a small object.

5. Drop your efforts to the base of the head, where it meets the neck. Knead this area, using firm upward presses with your thumbs. Work your way behind the ears, using the same repetitive upward and forward motion.

6. When you arrive at the temples, use the outside of your thumbs—primarily the knuckle where the thumb and hand meet—to provide firm, circular massage.

7. Switching to the knuckle bone in the middle of your thumbs, massage the forehead. Push from the temples to the middle of the scalp and back downward again along the hairline.

8. After a while, change the path so that you're making this movement directly above the eyebrows.

9. Once again, using the knuckle closest to where the thumb meets the hand, return the movement to the middle of the forehead. Pull downward on either side of the face, sweeping past the area where the ear and head meet, across the jaw, and down the sides of the neck.

10. Repeat this step, this time running from the top of the middle of the forehead, between the eyes, and down the sides of the nose to the

chin. Take the time to focus on the mid-eyebrow area. Reflexology holds that pressing this point stimulates the pituitary gland, sometimes referred to as the "crystal room cavity of the spirit tongue."

11. End the massage by cupping the middle of the forehead with the palm of one hand, fingers facing up, for a few moments, sending loving energy into your partner's third-eye chakra, directly between the eyebrows.

The result: This activity promotes touch receptivity by relaxing the body. This is especially important for those with orgasmic difficulties, since relaxation helps to promote sexual response during more genital-focused activities. Acupressure stimulation of the third eye will stimulate and balance the endocrine system, particularly the pituitary gland.

This exercise can be repeated in the bathtub or shower as you and your lover wash each other's hair. The shampoo lather will make your massaging movements even easier. Brushing your lover's hair, especially when it's dry, can also feel really good and can promote bonding, since any grooming activity is usually regarded as quite personal.

The following exercise focuses more on the scalp's acupressure points and is a great alternative when you want to focus on energy flow.

◙ EXERCISE 9.2: *Awakening*

1. With your partner's head in your lap, cup the back of their head with your hands.

2. Place your fingertips in the little hollows where the neck and skull meet. These are the Gates of Consciousness points (see Figure 9.1 on the next page); they allow energy to flow, making sex glorious.

3. Gradually increase the pressure.

4. Take the side of your partner's head into your hands and press into these points as you slowly tilt the head backward.

5. Now slowly move it forward. As you perform these movements, keep your breath in unison with your partner's.

6. Repeat the same movements, this time with the head in the center position (neither tilted forward nor back), pressing the large hollow

at the base of the skull—the medulla, sexual reflexology's Yui-Gen (also known as the cranial pump; see Figure 9.1).

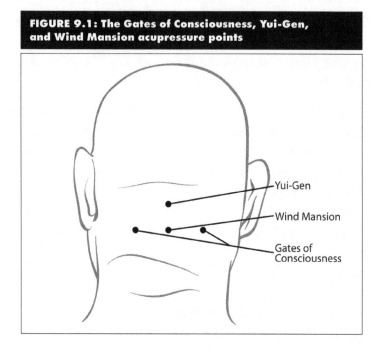

FIGURE 9.1: The Gates of Consciousness, Yui-Gen, and Wind Mansion acupressure points

7. Using the middle fingers of both hands, apply pressure on the medulla to activate the Wind Mansion acupressure point (see Figure 9.1); at the same time, slowly pull the head toward you, elongating the neck's vertebrae.

8. Grasping the head at the jaw, gently pull the head toward you so that the neck muscles are stretched.

9. Throughout this exercise, try to breathe together using long, slow breaths.

The result: These moves will help to increase your lover's circulation and awaken the senses. Furthermore, stimulating the Gates of Consciousness points during sex by holding them will heighten your lover's senses and consciousness, producing a natural high, especially if your partner is breathing deeply, eyes rolled upward and eyebrows raised. Activating the

Wind Mansion will open all spiritual senses and will also benefit the eyes, ears, nose, and throat.

The next exercise is one more way to both relax and stimulate your lover, and it takes less time than the preceding two exercises. Still, avoid rushing through it.

❡ EXERCISE 9.3: *The Third-Eye Chakra Press*

1. Gently press on the center of your lover's forehead, about an inch below the hairline, using the middle bone of your middle finger. Maintain the pressure on this point for one minute.

2. Rotate your fingers onto your partner's temples; hold this position for thirty seconds.

3. Tell your lover to concentrate on the growing sensation in their groin. As you focus your partner's attention, they will be better able to relish any feel-good sensations.

4. End this exercise with a pressed, lingering kiss on the area of the Third Eye (directly between the eyebrows; see Figure 9.2 on the next page).

The result: This move will allow for the release of tension and will increase the flow of sexual excitement.

Any time your partner's head can be reached during sex play, try stimulating the four acupressure points on the scalp—the Posterior Summit, One Hundred Meeting, Anterior Summit, and Penetrating Heaven—to open intuition and body wisdom and to connect with the universal flow. To find these points, start with those along the midline of the skull. Feel for the hollow area that is located toward the back of the center of the top of the head. This is the One Hundred Meeting point. The Posterior Summit is one thumb-width behind this point, and the Anterior Summit is one thumb-width in front of it. The Penetrating Heaven point is one thumb-width outward from the center of the top of the head, directly upward from the back of the ears. Working this part of the scalp also works the crown chakra.

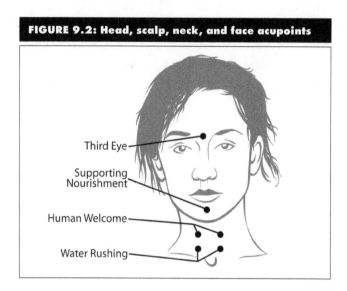

FIGURE 9.2: Head, scalp, neck, and face acupoints

Third Eye

Supporting Nourishment

Human Welcome

Water Rushing

The Neck

Sensual neck play symbolizes two people's relationship as lovers. The neck is a very personal, erotic part of the body because it is so sensitive, is very responsive to different temperatures and sensations, and can be ticklish. Not surprisingly, the neck contains meridians connected directly to the sacrum and pelvis, two points for sexual awakening. Furthermore, whether or not they're aware of it, people are quite protective of their necks. Despite the visibility and accessibility of the neck, most people allow very few others to touch this most intimate part of their bodies, which is yet another reason why it becomes such a hot spot when touched. A gesture as simple as kissing your beloved on the neck before parting for a few hours can reinforce your bond and indicate there's more intimacy to come later.

While basically any kissing, licking, nibbling, squeezing, and sucking of the neck area can feel good, having a stimulation game plan never hurts. (Note: Since men have thicker skin, a firmer touch is often needed to provide adequate stimulation.) Pulling up on any cluster of hair, travel down the nape of the neck, gently caressing and kissing it. Exhale purposefully while planting wet kisses, especially along the hairline. Blowing on this area will cause your lover's nerves to stand on end—if they aren't already! As things become more heated, use your whole mouth and suck (it's up to the both of you if you want to leave a mark). Stop every now and then and suck an area with your mouth before exhaling warm air from your lungs. This will relax any neck tension and will literally help to heat things up, with your lover's body becoming warmer. With your tongue, make swirling motions, gently massaging the area. On occasion, lovingly bite the neck.

A neck and shoulder massage, using your hands or a vibrating device, is always a welcome way to seduce your lover. If you're in the bathtub, use a washcloth or sponge to provide extra friction as you massage (this is especially pleasant because people usually have trouble accessing hard-to-reach spots by themselves). As you work your hands around the neck and shoulders, be aware that the thyroid glands, located on both sides of the throat a couple of inches below the earlobes and just behind the jawbone, hold sexual energy. Chinese medicine teaches that stimulating the thyroid gland—which also, by the way, houses the throat chakra—stimulates the sexual organs, and vice versa. Speaking the truth prevents the compromising of this energy center. Sexual reflexology says that gently massaging or kissing this part of the throat energy center (Hsuan Chi) with your fingertips frees up libidinal energy and increases sexual response. For women in particular, such stimulation increases sex drive and breast size. Furthermore, the Human Welcome and Water Rushing points are located on the sides of the throat toward the front, about one finger width apart, along major arteries (see Figure 9.2). Being careful not to press them simultaneously or too firmly, kiss or suck on them to heighten your lover's erotic experience and to enhance your harmony with the cosmos's natural forces.

The Ears

A person's ears can be *really* sensitive to touch. This is because there are a number of nerve endings in and around the ears. So as you stroke, kiss, nibble, lick, and pull at your partner's ears, be sure to use care. Lightly lick your lover's earlobes, tracing them with the wet tip of your tongue. Take them into your mouth and press them between your lips, massaging them lightly. Take the lobe between your teeth for light biting, or graze your teeth against the skin. Work your way into the ear, massaging the outer part with your lips before tracing the inside edges with your tongue. If your lover likes it, you can explore the inner part of the ear canal with lit-tle tongue-flicking motions. You can also softly blow on the area. Pay at-tention to your lover's responses; not everybody is crazy about these ac-tivities.

Every now and then, catch your breath, breathing hot air onto your lover's ear, especially the back of it. With your tongue, trace tiny circles around the dip behind the ear. If your tongue and mouth tire, put your thumbs to work, pressing them into the opening of your partner's ears. Massage the ear's inner skin. Gently pull and tug at the earlobes and outer ear, always keeping in mind that the ears hold some of the acupressure love points. Traditional Chinese medicine maintains that the ear is packed with over 120 acupressure points that, when touched, send sexual energy throughout the body, including into the genital region.

As you're performing these ear-pleasing actions (and since it so often goes without saying), don't forget the role of sound in eroticizing love-making. Many kinds of music, rhythmic sounds (like drumbeats), whis-pering, chimes, bells, chanting, murmured endearments, or dirty talk can make things steamier. A lover's singing, humming, exhaling, and paying compliments—even making satisfied noises like "Grrr"—can reinforce attraction and adoration. Likewise, an occasional silence that allows for sexy sounds such as rubbing skin, the crinkling of sheets, and a lover's breathing and sighing is way hot.

The following exercise helps you to connect with your lover, allowing both of you to listen to each other's sounds. Take your time as you move through each of the steps, soaking up the experience of merging.

◈ EXERCISE 9.4: *Merging Sound*

1. Have one partner lie on their back, knees bent.

2. The other partner should lie on their back on top of the bottom part-ner, both facing upward.

3. The top partner's head falls back over the bottom partner's left shoulder so that the top partner's right ear and the bottom partner's left ear are in alignment. (Or reverse things so that the top partner's left ear and the bottom partner's right ear are aligned.)

4. Each partner uses one hand to cover their outer ear.

5. Close your eyes and listen to your breaths.

6. Make sounds, feeling them resonate within each other.

7. Bottom partner: Use your free hand to stimulate the top partner's breasts, belly button, or genitals, paying particular attention to any acupressure points you have access to.

Result: This exercise helps lovers to stay connected through experiencing their sound sense as one.

The Eyelids

Eyelids are easily one of the most underrated, ignored areas of the body in terms of their capacity to provide sensual stimulation. This is understandable since people are often afraid of poking somebody in the eye or otherwise inflicting discomfort on this delicate area. But sensory exploration of the eyelid can be done without causing harm.

◀ EXERCISE 9.5: *Eyelid Erotica*

You can provide the eyelid with unusual sensations by touching the tip of your nose to it. As you pull away, brush the eyelashes with your nose tip, carefully and slowly breathing air out through your nose for a tickling effect. Next, kiss the eyebrows, massaging them with your lips. As you move your way downward across your lover's closed eye, brush the eyelid with the warm, wet inside of your lower lip, softly soothing the lid's delicate skin. Replace your lips with a warm finger or thumb, which will make the feelings of sensuality and closeness linger. A partner's trust in your ability to handle this area so lovingly is endearing. Gently explore the eye sockets and lids. Run your thumbs softly over the eyeballs and over the corner crease. Make light massaging circles at the corners, moving out toward the temples. Use this opportunity to really look at your lover's face, taking in everything you adore about it.

To wrap up your exploration efforts, first rub your hands together to create warmth. Sit behind your partner, perhaps with their head in your lap, and then lay a hand over each closed eyelid, cupping the area for a couple of minutes. This act of tenderness will feel amazing to your partner. Seal your efforts with a kiss in the middle of your lover's forehead.

When you practice this exercise another time, make it memorable by creating different sensations. Instead of producing warmth with your hands to end the experience, use an eye pillow, eye mask, eye cream, or eye gel (L'Occitane makes a good one for producing an awakening effect). Any such activities will relieve tired eyes and tension and leave your partner feeling revived and much friskier!

The Eyes

Sight plays an enormous role in arousal and attraction, whether you're eyeing your partner or other erotic stimuli. When people first fall in love, they spend oodles of time gazing into each other's eyes. Considered by many, particularly those involved in Chinese medicine, to be the windows to the soul, the eyes signal sexual interest and love. This is one of the reasons why tantric sex is very much about maintaining eye contact with your lover during lovemaking as a way to stay connected and feed each other energy. Try to stay mindful of the role of the eyes as a hot spot so you won't take them for granted when engaging in sex play.

Since the eyes are so central to the processing of erotic stimulation, covering them often makes sex play that much more exciting. Blindfolded lovers feel enjoyably vulnerable and titillated because the rest of their senses come to life. What a person can't see can become more arousing than what can be seen because it creates an exciting unknown (as well as providing a great way to fantasize about the unknown!). Also, the partner without the blindfold gets off on the power they hold over the helpless one as they see their partner in a whole new light. Don't be afraid to give the exercises and activities described in this book an entirely different flavor by using a blindfold. On occasion, try an activity with both partners blindfolded or make it an Arabian night: Wrap a scarf around your face so that it covers the lower half. Seeing only your eyes makes you mysterious; it can be like having sex with a totally different person!

Although valuable for new lovers, the following exercise is especially important if you and your partner need to reconnect, or if your passionate love has cooled, or if you want to rediscover how you used to turn each other on. Known as soul gazing, this practice transmits a wealth of sexual energy between lovers; some people attain orgasm simply by gazing at their beloved.

◀ EXERCISE 9.6: *Soul Gazing*

1. Standing or sitting, face your partner and gaze softly into each other's eyes. Make sure that your bodies are aligned.

2. Pay more attention to your partner's left eye, which in tantric practice is considered the receiving eye.

3. Stay relaxed, and blink as you need to. Don't stare intensely.

4. Feel yourself melting more deeply into the union between the two of you.

5. Remain conscious of whatever feelings surface while being careful not to get distracted by any one thought.

6. Tune in to your body's reactions, and try to remain relaxed and comfortable.

7. Continue for as long as both of you want to.

EXERCISE 9.6: Soul gazing

You can vary this activity by putting one hand on your partner's face as their right hand rests on your heart, and by placing your other hand on your left thigh. The next time you're intimate, try to maintain this type of soul gazing during thrusting, if the position allows it. The results will be explosive.

Results: This exercise builds trust, promotes relaxation, and helps lovers to merge.

We could devote an entire book to visual sexual stimulation. Scores of works already address the topics of erotic art, pornography, and the like. You can use any number of visual stimuli to get turned on—for example, sex flicks, literary lesbian erotica, etc.—but we're going to focus here on the importance of color. The next time you don lingerie or buy silky bed sheets or paint your bedroom or change your lightbulbs, consider incorporating the following colors to totally pump up the titillation factor:

* *Lavender* signifies fantasy, romance, and imagination
* *Pink* is linked to commitment, compassion, and companionship
* *Purple* is all about passion and spirituality (and is related to the crown chakra)
* *Red* screams pleasure and vigor (and represents the root and heart chakras)

Envisioning these colors as you make love will trigger emotional reactions that will bring you even more into the moment.

Give new meaning to keeping the lights on during sex. Grab a flashlight, get under the covers, and have fun exploring each other. Shining a spotlight on your own and your lover's most precious parts is one way to show off your bodies and see them in a whole new light—literally.

The Nose

The nose is a major source of eroticism for a number of overlooked reasons beyond its role in smell. First, the nose is central to tantric practice because it's the entrance to the breath, the life force known as **prana.**

Fully and deeply filling your lungs with breath during intimacy allows your body to relax, calms your body when it is stressed and tense, and helps you to better focus your mind; plus, it enhances your senses and mood and energizes your body. All of this leads to more satisfying sex.

Second, the tip of the nose is believed to hold great energy potential. According to tantric practice, it lies on the meridian that connects to the root chakra. Touching it sends energy flowing through that meridian, revitalizing the base of the pelvic area. If you trace your lover's meridian path from the tip of the nose down along the front of the abdomen to the root chakra and then back to the nose, you create a total energy circuit that awakens sexual desire. Give it a try!

Third, while odors can turn a lover on—or off—they do something equally important. They leave an association imprint in your memory. If a specific event is associated with a certain smell, when reencountering that smell, a person is more likely to recall not only the event, but also, just as importantly, the feelings that went along with it.

Aromatherapy, the use of essential oils to trigger specific effects or results, is especially effective at helping people to associate luscious smells with erotic moments. Certain scents are valuable in increasing attraction and enhancing sex play. If you use essential oils (oils that give plants their characteristic fragrance or flavor), incense, scented candles, massage oils, or scented soaps in your boudoir, give special consideration to the following fragrances, especially those that correspond with the chakras (see Chapter 1):

✳ Earthy, pungent *patchouli* relieves stress, increases sexual energy, and clears distracting thoughts.

✳ *Ginger* promotes circulation, increases body warmth, and stimulates sexual interest and energy.

✳ *Jasmine,* associated with the third-eye chakra, can enhance romantic feelings and increase sexual interest and energy.

✳ *Peppermint* promotes circulation.

✳ *Ylang ylang,* which comes from a tropical Asian flower, has euphoric, aphrodisiac qualities, increasing blood pressure as well as sexual interest and energy.

Other great scents include white musk (the crown chakra's scent), orange blossom (the sacral chakra's scent), rose (the heart chakra's scent), carnation, amber, cinnamon, sage, sandalwood, eucalyptus, wood, mint, floral, neroli, cedarwood, and vanilla. Smells that have been found to increase penile blood flow in particular include freshly baked cinnamon buns, a combination of fresh doughnuts and pumpkin pie or licorice, and a combination of lavender, pumpkin, cinnamon, and nutmeg, so you might want to consider what you have for breakfast.

Know that you don't always need these specific scents to get things going in terms of aroma. You can spice things up by blindfolding your partner and stimulating the nose with handier fragrances, ones you might have around the house, such as red wine, orange peels, and chocolate. Even easier, use each other's body smells. Try closing your eyes and letting your nose lead you, breathing in the different arousing scents your lover's body produces around the armpits, on the scalp, and near the groin. Have your love do the same to you.

Whether or not you have had sex, get under the covers and simply breathe, enjoying whatever smells await you. Fresh, clean sheets will have an invigorating effect, while sheets that have seen some sleep and/or sex action are likelier to offer up familiar scents that are calming and stimulating—that is, if you like your partner's scent. Smelling your partner's hair, scalp, neck, and face can also be a turn-on that reinforces your bond with your lover. (However, a smell that's a turn-off may make you want to reconsider the relationship.)

As you massage your lover's head, neck, and shoulders, use the power of smell to further enhance your seduction and relaxation efforts, particularly by using a lotion or shampoo containing any of the scents listed above.

Since breathing fully and deeply is such an important component of better sex, practice the following exercise on a regular basis, with or without your partner, to get more in tune with your breath and to better control it during any kind of lovemaking.

◙ EXERCISE 9.7: *Tuning In to Your Breath*

1. Sit tall in a comfortable, cross-legged position.

2. Place your right hand lightly over your heart and your left hand over your abdomen.

3. If it helps, close your eyes.

4. Breathe in steadily, feeling fresh air enter your nostrils.

5. In your mind, follow this breath down into your chest and belly.

6. Breathe out through your nose, feeling the warmth of the air leaving your nostrils.

7. Repeat the breath, only this time feeling the rise and fall of your body against your hands.

8. Inhale slowly for five counts, letting the breath sink deeply into your lower belly and chest.

9. Hold your inhalation for five counts.

10. Exhale slowly for five counts.

11. Hold your breath out for five counts.

12. Repeat until you find yourself able to do this comfortably and without distraction.

Results: Practicing conscious breathing on a regular basis will help you to breathe more fully during sex, allowing you to immerse yourself in the experience as you channel the breath to energize your body and spread your orgasmic response. Breathing also increases your sensual awareness and pleasure, fortifies your sexual reproductive system, opens your heart, stabilizes your emotional intimacy, enhances your vigor, and makes you present in the moment, enabling you to give and receive more fully.

When focusing on your breath—or when refocusing on it if your mind strays—silently say the following to yourself:

◉ *"It is the breath that brings me vitality."*

◉ *(As you inhale) "My inhalation nourishes and energizes my body."*

◉ *(As you exhale) "I am purified."*

❦ EXERCISE 9.8: *Breathing Your Way to O*

Given the role of breath in climax, try this breathing technique during sex to produce a bigger, more intense orgasm: Inhale deeply and steadily through your nose. Imagine the air filling every part of your body, energizing every cell. Then, exhale as slowly as you can through your mouth. Continue to take these long breaths as your heart rate gets faster and sex play becomes more charged, till you explode with an ethereal orgasm.

Lips

The lips are among the body's most sensitive spots since the mucous membranes that comprise them have a dense supply of nerve endings; specifically, touch and pressure receptors. Since the skin of the lips is very thin, these nerves lie close to the surface, making them more responsive to stimulation. As we become increasingly aroused, our lips become more fully engorged with blood, further heightening sensitivity. Sexual reflexology teaches that in deep (otherwise known as soul or French) kissing, the tongue reflects and connects lovers' hearts via each partner's Functional and Governor channels, creating a complete circuit of energy flow.

Most humans love being kissed. Our brain pays nearly twice as much attention to the lips as it does to the genitals. Consider how often you unconsciously lick or bite your lips as you're thinking. Think about what a tease it is when somebody kisses you all over—how good the wetness, suction, and pressure feel. Think about how tantalizing *not* being kissed can be, especially when your love purposefully avoids your lips, kissing every other part of your face and neck in order to build anticipation. Think about how amazing it feels to receive an incredible kiss versus a mediocre one and how much this can play into your decision to want to go farther physically with a potential lover.

It is important to always give good attention to the act of kissing since it is one of the top ways to get turned on. Since some couples neglect this type of sex play after being together for a while, strive to pucker up while you're working your other moves (e.g., as you run your hands all over your partner's body) in order to take things up a level. Make sure you mix up your kissing techniques every time you embrace, depending on the mood. Plunging straight into the mouth with your tongue may have its moments, but it gets really old if that's all you do. Vary the intensity of your kisses, making them sometimes gentle and grazing, sometimes lip-lock passionate. Take turns being the active and passive kisser.

According to Eastern thought, the lips are related to the genitals. Tantric teachings hold that a nerve-like connection exists between a woman's upper lip and her clitoris. When she's kissed, the sensations run along the channel from her lip through her body to her clit. Having her visualize this flow of sexual energy during the kiss will help to enhance these sensations even more fully. Likewise, orally caressing her clitoris sends sensations through her body to her upper lip. By licking and sucking the lips of her mouth, you can stimulate her sexual organs. If you keep this in mind while you're kissing, your movements may take on a whole new life.

Visualize how the various ways you use your mouth are actually stirring your lover's loins. Lick your partner's lips as though you were lapping whipped cream out of a mug of hot chocolate, or lick your lover's lower lip softly and then suck it into your mouth. When you move to French kissing, open your mouths together, but don't swap tongues right away. Pause in order to relish the anticipation. Cradle your lover's head as you finally twist tongues.

If up to now you've taken lips for granted, you may find that attending to them is a sexually stimulating experience of its own. Whether it's the first time or the ten thousandth time you've kissed your adored one, consider approaching the act in a whole new way by using the following exercise.

◙ EXERCISE 9.9: *Lip Exploration*

1. Trace the outline of your lover's mouth with your fingertips.

2. Press against your partner's lips with your own.

3. Move your lips around your beloved's mouth, every now and then moving to other areas of the face.

4. One partner kisses the upper lip while the other kisses the lower lip. Use your tongue to stimulate the area where upper lip meets gum.

5. Try touching each other's teeth with your tongues.

6. Take your lover's lower lip into your mouth, and using the tip of your tongue, playfully lick the indented area where your partner's outer lip and chin meet before moving back upward for a full lip lock.

7. Kiss the indentation midway between your lover's lower lip and chin. The center of this area holds the Supporting Nourishment point (see Figure 9.2 on page 118), which relaxes the facial muscles and enhances awareness of the sexual energy around the lips.

Results: This exercise fully engages all of the lip's nerve endings and allows partners to connect.

❋ EXERCISE 9.10: *Kissing Two Lips at Once*

In this exercise, the recipient is a woman.

1. Gently take her upper lip between your lips and begin to suck it so that your lower lip lightly rubs her mouth's frenulum (the tiny bit of connective tissue located inside the mouth between upper lip and gum).

2. On occasion, run your tongue across this area.

The result: According to Dr. Gloria Brame, the frenulum is considered a direct channel to her clitoris. When it's stimulated, some women experience a clitoral orgasm.

The Power of Lips

Research has indicated that the size of an individual's lips plays a key role in determining whether they are sexually attractive to other people. Basically, the bigger the better, but too big is generally deemed unattractive. Medium-sized lips are considered better on men than either too small or too large, and women's lips are considered sexier if full, red, and warm, which indicates receptivity and expressiveness. (Think about how someone's lips flush, becoming darker and fuller, when they're pleased to see you.) Pursing your lips is not a positive signal and, in sexual terms, is taken as indicating disinterest.

The Tongue

It practically goes without saying that the tongue's role in attraction and seduction includes its ability to taste and to stimulate as well as its high receptivity to touch. In conjunction with the sense of smell, the tongue's ability to detect the mix of salt and sweet on a lover's body plays a part in turning lovers on.

Throughout this book I have discussed the tongue's wetness, warming and lubricating effects, and range of movements, such as presses and strokes. I would now like to suggest using this muscle to vary the nature of your strokes as you stimulate any hot spot. As you explore erogenous zones, alternate between using the top of your tongue and then its underside. This will heighten excitement by adding new elements to your touch.

Humans have long utilized their taste buds to make sex an even more appetizing experience. With or without a blindfold, try offering your sweetheart any of the following oral aphrodisiacs: chocolate, fruit (e.g., grapes, orange blossoms, mango), wine, champagne, raw seafood (e.g., oysters, clams), any food containing spices like black pepper, chili peppers, or mandrake (these boost the body's heat, making you feel more turned on). As you satiate your partner's animal appetite, don't be shy about giving him or her a taste of yourself every now and then, whether it's your luscious lips, your nipples (perhaps dipped in powdered sugar or honey), or other parts of your body.

Beyond its value when it comes to taste and stimulation, the tongue is viewed as a switch that connects the two channels in the body that circulate chi (energy). Sexual reflexology holds that when touched to the roof of the mouth just behind the teeth, the tongue completes a circuit of energy flow, allowing energy to travel up the spine and continue down the front of the body. This current, known as the Microcosmic Orbit, provides the body's cells with the energy needed to grow, heal, and function, ultimately improving sexual functioning. Furthermore, according to Taoism, the tongue is an energetic extension of the heart and is strongly connected to the sexual center. Exercising the tongue, as described in the following activity, helps to open the heart and activate sexual energy.

⟡ EXERCISE 9.11: *Titillating Tongue Action*

Place the tip of your tongue between your front teeth and the inside of your upper lip. Circle it in a counterclockwise direction downward to the inside of the lower lip and back up; complete up to forty repetitions. Change directions.

To activate your heart and sexual center as a part of foreplay or sex, perform the following exercise.

⟡ EXERCISE 9.12: *Tongue Slide*

Vigorously slide your tongue back and forth against your upper palate, massaging it up to forty times. Feel the heat move from the roof of your mouth to the rest of your body.

The Brain

Believe it or not, your brain is the primary source of the Big O. The brain is by far the largest, most orgasmic hot spot in the entire human body. Consider the following evidence: Some people with spinal-cord injuries that make them unable to feel anything below the waist still report experiencing orgasm. **Nocturnal orgasms**, which can happen to either sex (they're called "wet dreams" when they happen to males, because they usually result in ejaculation), occur as you dream because your brain gets your body so turned on that your body goes through the entire sexual-response cycle—even without your having experienced any physical stimulation. This is possible because the brain houses your main sexual-response center. The limbic system, in the central region, holds three key areas: (1) the amygdala, which controls emotional states and affects how we interpret sexual stimuli; (2) the hypothalamus, which regulates sexual behavior and expression and mediates how we feel pleasure; and (3) the septum, a pleasure pathway. Furthermore, the brain's cerebral cortex is in charge of our ability to speak, learn, think, perceive, and make choices, including governing our sexual fantasies, daydreams, and memories.

The brain is also involved in sexual arousal, releasing endorphins when a person experiences intense physical activity, heavy breathing, and sexual stimulation. Endorphins are responsible for the pleasurable sensations we experience when we become aroused to the point that we experience an altered state of consciousness.

In Taoism, the center of the brain is connected to the uterus and prostate gland. In fact, all of the body's sexual organs (ovaries, uterus, testicles, and prostate gland) are closely connected to the brain, particularly the pineal gland, a.k.a. the "enlightenment gland" or "gland of direction," which sits beneath the crown chakra. Taoists believe that circulating sexual energy down to the sacrum and then back up to the brain increases brain memory.

Yet while the brain does so much for our sexual functioning and response, it can also foil its own efforts. The brain can literally play head games with us in the sack, acting as friend or foe. Many performance issues and problems prove to be psychological in nature. Things like negative thoughts (conscious or not), memories of bad experiences, and spectatoring (watching and evaluating yourself or your partner during sex) act as some of the many mental barriers to mind-blowing sex. The way we think and feel about ourselves as human beings and as partners and lovers has a direct influence on our bodies and our brain activity during sexual goings-on. For example, if you believe that something is attainable, then it's likelier to happen. Likewise, if you believe that you are unable to experience something (for example, a climax), this mindset can have a strong negative influence on your physical ability to do so. Performance pressure makes matters even worse, causing lovers to worry that they're not good enough in the sack and to put pressure on themselves to "achieve." The phrase "achieve orgasm" is probably one of the worst terms ever used in sexology. It turns sex play into something goal-oriented instead of encouraging lovers simply to be in the moment, relaxing and fully enjoying intimacy. Many people's minds have been held hostage by the notion that sex isn't good enough unless it involves a certain result, usually orgasm.

Although every person's problems and every couple's issues require a personalized solution, one thing every couple can do is to take the pressure off of themselves to perform and respond like a rock star. Simply agree that neither partner is required to climax, since a performance-oriented focus on orgasm can be unconstructive and anxiety provoking, making you tense and distressed during intimacy. A person can become anxious just thinking about it! Instead, fill your mind with a wealth of sexual images, thoughts, and feelings. Doing so will help you to connect more fully with your inner sexual self and develop a deeper understanding of your erotic nature. It will also free you up to enjoy yourself and your partner that much more. By eliminating expectations, you release inhibitions that may have otherwise prevented you from exploring new moves, techniques, positions, and touches for fear they would ruin orgasmic response. With this changed mindset, you allow yourself to focus on simply enjoying the intimacy—and you may end up discovering something quite unexpectedly erogenous.

Sexual experiences that reaffirm that we are sexual beings are a turn-on. Whereas watching yourself during sex, for example, can be a visual turn-on, it also reminds you that you're desirable, erotic, and sexual—beliefs that serve as aphrodisiacs. It's your thought process that makes an experience sexy, so the next time your sex life needs a little boost, sit with your lover at the edge of the bed or in a chair in front of a full-length mirror. Both of you should face the mirror, so that you can see your reflection as one lover enters the other. The bottom partner can further enhance the action by putting their hands under the top partner's thighs and lifting them up and apart for a breathtaking view. You'll be amazed at how your body—and mind—react.

As touched upon earlier, sexual fantasies are one of the many ways your brain is involved in sexual functioning. Fantasies range from having a crush on somebody to narrating a complete story plot in your imagination to having dreams that get you off in your sleep. Whether a substitute for sex, a part of foreplay, or a way to breathe new excitement into your sex life, fantasy is a great tool to use if you're in a monogamous relationship, practicing safer sex, or simply want to be titillated without limits.

Fantasies can be as tame or as hard-core as you want them to be. After all, you're the director and this is a private viewing, so who besides you has to know what's going on? Some things people like to fantasize about when masturbating, making love with another, or sharing fantasies with a partner include new sexual positions, being intimate in unusual locations, forced sex (even if it's not desired in real life), bondage, being found irresistible, sex with a new lover, partaking in a deviant behavior, group sex, watching others have sex, and being the dominant partner during sex. As yet another way to eroticize lovemaking, fantasies can fuel role-playing. Couples can pretend to change gender roles (sometimes including crossdressing), pretend to have sex in a place where they might get caught, pretend to have sex with a sex worker, pretend to have sex with a virgin, and pretend to have sex with a taboo partner. As long as play-acting your fantasies remains consensual and safe, it is a healthy, natural part of a sexual relationship that never grows tiresome.

Keeping your head's hot spots engaged during foreplay and sex is an important part of helping you stay in the moment and in helping you feel completely lost in all of the sensations. All too often, lovers will abandon head action for the below-the-belt region, never to travel north again. Paying attention to erogenous zones all over each other's head and neck allows the two of you to feel connected for a longer period of time and helps to create an overall mind-body-soul experience.

10

The All-Over Hot Spots

D o you ever feel sexy all over, with your whole body coming alive, feeling tingly, and craving sex? You want sex. You exude sex. You are sex. And you're covered in it from head to toe. Your skin is your largest erogenous zone. As your biggest sense organ, your skin is made up of millions of nerve fibers, with the skin of adults containing between six and seven hundred thousand receptor cells that are able to detect sensation. Consequently, your brain is devoted to touch more than it is to any of your other senses. There are also about five million strands of hair on the body, which enhance your body's sense of touch even more fully. Basically, your body is one big hot spot, but we're going to break things down, getting a little naughty as we consider each individual area.

Although any part of a person's body—any square inch of skin—can trigger an erotic response, some places are known to elicit these sorts of reactions more than others. As we examine each of these hot spots more closely, consider how you could stimulate them while simultaneously arousing other parts of the body. Imagine what combinations might work best for you or your lover. Think of all the ways you could express what you like best, whether by simply saying "Touch me here" with a wink and a seductive smile; by giving a silent demonstration, your gaze locked with your lover's; or by taking your lover's hand and pressing their fingers into a spot just the way you like it. It's important not to overlook the skin spots when you're having a roll in the hay and you become caught up in the rush of the genitals, because simultaneously stimulating any of these other areas can make for the wildest, best sex ever and a more total-body sexual experience.

The Shoulders

Shoulders are always good for kissing, snuggling, massaging. One of the best sensations in the world is that of a loved one holding you close, as you bury your head into their neck. From the time we're babies, we appreciate shoulders. Whether they're our shoulders or somebody else's, we like to take care of them, massaging them, kneading them, caressing them. Practically nobody turns down a good shoulder rub. How would you like to be able to massage this hot spot so well that people beg for you to work their shoulders?

Stimulating two acupressure points on either shoulder, the Shoulder Well and Heavenly Rejuvenation, can relieve stress and irritability, making the recipient even more charged up for sex. The Shoulder Well points are located on the highest point of the top of the shoulder muscle, one inch outward from the base of the lower neck (see Figure 10.1 on the next page). The Heavenly Rejuvenation points are located on the upper back, half an inch directly below the Shoulder Well (see Figure 10.1). Press firmly into these points while either hugging your partner or while standing behind them, as you knead their neck and shoulder to relieve tension. (A pregnant woman requires a lighter touch.) Be sure to curve your fingers so that they hook the points, while both partners breathe simultaneously, exhaling the tension with the slow massage.

The Arms

If you're after some sizzling sex play, know that the underside of a person's arm is quite sensitive to touch. Racing your fingertips lightly over this area while out on the town or as a part of foreplay can do wonders. During sex, throw your partner's arms up over their head and run your

FIGURE 10.1: The Shoulder Well, Heavenly Rejuvenation, and Elegant Mansion acupressure points

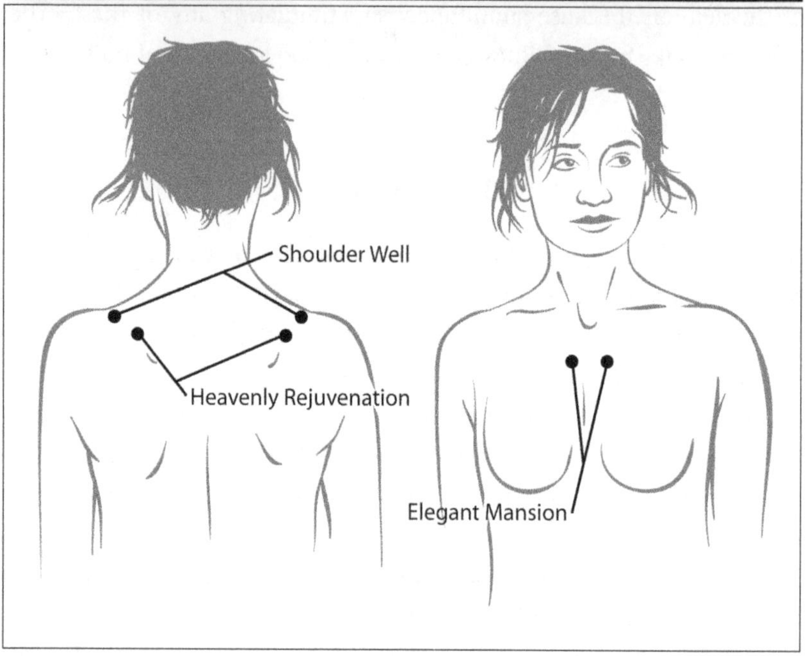

fingertips down the exposed area to the armpit. At the wrist, begin gently nibbling your way downward, skillfully exhaling in specific locations along the way. Pay extra attention to kissing and blowing on the inside of the elbow. At the armpit, inhale. Lick. A musky underarm smell has been proven arousing by scientific research, so breathe it in if it's enticing to you. An alternative to this move could involve massaging refrigerated moisturizer into the pit, which will raise goose bumps all over your love's body.

The Collarbone

Although the collarbone is one of the sexiest parts of a person's body, with all of the excitement generated by the arms and shoulders, it's easy to overlook. But the sensuous, muscle-relaxing, rejuvenating effect afforded by working the tension-prone collarbone area deserves notice. Press into the Elegant Mansion acupressure point, located in the depression below the collarbone's protrusion (see Figure 10.1). As you perform the following exercise, you're likely to hear unexpected "ahhhs."

❧ EXERCISE 10.1: *Collarbone Stimulation*

1. Sit behind your partner.

2. With your thumb and first two fingers, starting at the inside end of the collarbone, slowly and firmly press along it, moving outward. Repeat this movement several times.

3. With the heel of your hand, repeat this massaging motion, again traveling outward, finishing by pushing into the indented area where the collarbone and shoulder meet.

4. Repeat on the other side.

5. With your thumb and forefinger, press into the indentations below the collarbone, massaging them thoroughly.

6. Repeat on the other side.

7. Using the heel of your hand, massage just the upper part of the breast. (Many massage therapists avoid this area, especially in women, for fear of seeming too personal.)

8. Move the heel of your hand to continue this massage on the upper center of the chest, which will stimulate the Shan Chung (thymus gland), the rejuvenation center located behind the sternum, which runs the body's immune center.

If at all possible, try working the hot spots in this chapter before moving to the genitals, as stimulation of the penis or vagina can detract from the pleasure sensations the rest of the body has to offer. Subtle sensations, like licking a lover's armpit, are going to feel totally different if libidinal desires are postponed and if you make these skin spots the sole focus. Naturally, these spots can also help to spread genital sensations during sex if stimulated properly at the same time.

The Back

Your back is a wonderland of erogenous potential. With the practically endless variations available, how can you ever get tired of giving or receiving a back massage? While nearly everybody loves having any part of their back massaged, the following are some areas worth paying a little more attention to

❊ the small of the back, which is full of nerve endings and an area where stress accumulates. Massaging this region also helps increase blood flow to the pelvic area, so orgasm is likely to be heightened.

❊ the sacral curve, located at the base of the spine. Pressing your thumbs into the muscles on either side of the vertebrae draws blood into the groin, increasing the energy that flows into the pelvis, hence enhancing arousal.

❊ the dimple just above each butt cheek. Pushing and pulling the skin of this area triggers genital movement, which causes a sexual feeling to spread up the spine.

When you give a massage, make sure that the space in which you are giving it is warm and draft free. Clean towels and pillows also make the experience that much more pleasant.

To give a killer back massage, you have to be willing to move. Don't get stuck in one place. It may be better at times to sit at your partner's head or to kneel at the side of their torso rather than sitting at their feet. Even if you're working a particular spot on your lover's body, doing so effectively may require a total-body response on your part. Don't be afraid to straddle your lover and to get your entire body into the act, rather than merely using your hands and arms.

Use a mixture of soft and hard moves; employ your fingers, palms, the edges of your hands, fists, soles, thumbs, finger pads, and elbows, changing the pressure as needed with each change in body part. Start out easy by applying light touches to any given spot, making sure it isn't too tender, before gradually applying more pressure, and always check in with your partner regarding what feels good. Movements may include long, rhythmic strokes, patting, hitting the skin as though it were a drum, compressing, kneading, rubbing, pinching, pressing, scraping, grasping, hammering with "karate-chop" motions, shaking, and vibrating. Here's a killer move: Grasp the skin, tugging it away from the spine before releasing it, especially at the sacrum area. This will help to open the spine and unblock the energy channel.

Experiment with different sensations. Use your tongue anywhere; for example, run it up the spine. Utilize your nails from time to time, scratching little circles all over your lover's back. Vary the pace. Use a variety of enhancements, such as massage oil, a feather, a paintbrush, a popsicle, or powder (e.g., Argo cornstarch, which goes on smoothly like oil).

No matter what you're doing or how you're doing it, be aware of the following acupressure and reflexology points that should receive extra attention:

❋ Sea of Vitality acupressure points lie on the lower back between the second and third lumbar vertebrae (two and four finger-widths away from the spine at waist level—i.e., in line with the belly button; see Figure 10.2 on the next page). These points store and foster physical and sexual energy, and govern the reproductive system. They are an area you can massage, but they are best pressed while hugging your partner. With one hand placed over the other on your lover's lower back, using fingertips on one side and the heel of the hand on the other, find and firmly squeeze the ropelike muscular cords on both sides of the lower back.

❋ The upper back houses four pairs of love points that can stimulate sexual energy, and these points are located between 1½ and 3 inches down the back on both sides of the spine (see Figure 10.2). The top points align with the second vertebrae down from the thoracic vertebra, the large bone that protrudes at shoulder level when the head bends forward; the bottom points line up with the lower part of the fifth thoracic vertebra. Using your fingertips, press each of the love points firmly for a few seconds, repeating regularly.

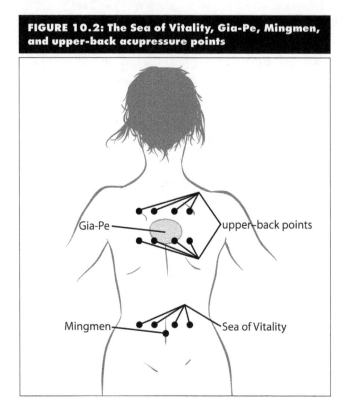

FIGURE 10.2: The Sea of Vitality, Gia-Pe, Mingmen, and upper-back acupressure points

❋ Gia-Pe is the name of a reflexology point located on the area of the back that is opposite the heart center (see Figure 10.2). As you hug your partner, press this area with the palm of one hand, while placing your other hand atop the bottom hand.

❋ The point known as the Mingmen (see Figure 10.2) is considered both a life gate for sexual energy and, in reflexology, the second center for male erection. It is located directly under the second lumbar vertebra, just below the back of the waist, and it should be pressed firmly with the fingertips.

The Sacrum

Although it is part of the lower back, the sacral area deserves special attention. Its sixteen acupressure points lie along the base of the spine in the sacrum's hollows (the large bony area at the base of the spine; see Figure

10.3). Pressing these points activates the sacral nerves, which in turn stimulates your partner's genitals. To stimulate these points, feel for slight indentations at the base of the spine, and firmly hold them with your fingertips. This may be done most easily when hugging or slow dancing, so it can be made an integral part of foreplay. As you hold your partner, gradually apply firm pressure to the points. Also, try placing the palm of one hand at the base of your lover's spine and firmly pressing it as you use your other hand to lightly touch other hot spots or as you press your pelvises together.

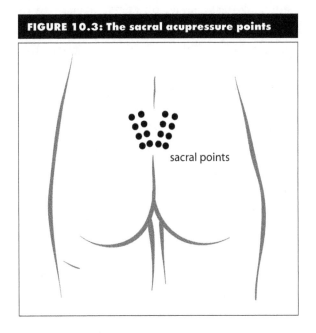

FIGURE 10.3: The sacral acupressure points

sacral points

Sexual reflexology views this area slightly differently. It holds that the sacral-coccygeal area can be stimulated and massaged at the top of one's butt crease; that is, at the tailbone. Sprinkled with eight love points (instead of sixteen), the sacrum can invite sexual arousal when a lover firmly presses into the small indentation at the base of the spine. The ninth point on the coccyx, the sacral pump, known as Chang-Chiang, can also be stimulated in this manner.

❧ EXERCISE 10.2: *Dirty Dancing*

Go dancing! It's the perfect opportunity to exercise your tailbone, hips, and lower back, which will relax and strengthen them. The more motion the sacrum experiences, the better the circulation in the sexual center. As you dance, take a wide stance, with your hands on your hips or in front of you. As you move, turning from the left to the right, breathe fully and deeply. Make sure you spiral the coccyx, sacrum, and hips separately from the upper torso (above the waist) and the legs, moving in every direction and extending your hips forward and back as much as possible. This will stretch and stimulate the sacral region's nerve fibers, activating the hormones of the testicles and prostate or of the ovaries and uterus. It will also help you to open up the genital area. Plus, dancing is a great way to flirt with your partner, get both of your heartbeats going, and touch and enjoy each other's bodies in a more sensual way.

The Womb and Vitals are two other acupressure points in this area, located one to two finger-widths outside of the sacrum, midway between the top of the hip bone and base of the buttocks (see Figure 2.1 on page 29). Pressing on these triggers activates the sacral nerve, thereby stimulating the genitals. You can use these points to arouse yourself or your partner during oral sex or intercourse.

Using a thin, flexible loofah on any of the hot spots covered in this chapter can offer a new kind of effect. After wetting the skin thoroughly with water or lubricant, begin massaging the chosen spot lightly. Follow this rough sensation with a smooth lick of your tongue.

The Abdomen

It's easy to home in on the navel and work your way downward, because the belly button is a natural bull's-eye for sex play. Rimming the navel with your tongue can produce surprising sensations that may prompt you to head further south. But before you do so, you should first kiss and massage the area below the breastbone. Doing so channels positive energy into the solar plexus chakra, helping to promote total-body sexual energy.

Sexual treasure seekers love the hairline trail running from navel to groin. It's there to be licked, nibbled, tickled, and gently pulled. Massaging this area gets the blood pumping since the action is happening so close to the groin. Such play becomes a tease.

The area through which this "treasure trail" passes, stretching from each hipbone to the groin, is known as the V-zone (see Figure 10.4). This erogenous zone is prime for sexual stimulation with simple finger caresses, kisses, and licks that may ultimately move to teasing the vulva or penis. Its crevices, the area where thigh meets pelvis, contain ligaments surrounded by nerve endings and covered with thin, sensitive skin—prime territory for heart-pumping action.

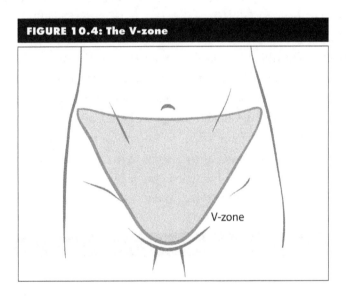

FIGURE 10.4: The V-zone

V-zone

The V-zone also houses a number of acupressure points. Using soft, light touches, you can stimulate the Gate of Origin, which lies directly above the bladder, or you can just rest your palm there, letting the energy flow from your hand into your lover's body. The sacral chakra, located below the navel on both sexes, is the area that houses most of a woman's sexual organs. When it is opened, women can more readily free their emotions, which enables them to reach out to and to feel others physically and sexually. Touching this area also stimulates your partner's sacred spot, the G-spot, from the outside, releasing sexual energy. In men, openness in this area translates into greater confidence in their ability to relate to their lover. Applying light pressure to the area as your lover breathes deeply will result in enhanced arousal.

Other points that are a must-know when stimulating the abdomen include

* the Sea of Intimacy acupressure points. Located two, three, and four finger-widths below the navel, on the line between the navel and pubic bone, these points can be pressed to restore, secure, and supplement sexual intimacy (see Figure 5.3 on page 80).

* seven reflexology love points that are closely tied to sexual well-being, collectively referred to as the Cinnabar Field, which are located in an area of the lower abdomen in front of the pubic bone. The points, which lie about an inch apart from one another, are as follows: Yin-Chiao (Sexual Crossroads—the major point in the Cinnabar Field), Chi-Hai (Sea Gate—a relatively major love point), Shih-Men (Stone Gate), Kuen-Yuan (Pass of Primacy), Chung-Chi (Ultimate Middle), Chu-Ku (the pubic bone), and the navel (or umbilicus) itself (see Figure 10.5). To work these points, lightly stroke or press each with your palm for three to five seconds. Release and repeat, perhaps using a hardened tongue point instead of your hand. Any type of stimulation of these points is believed to increase arousal.

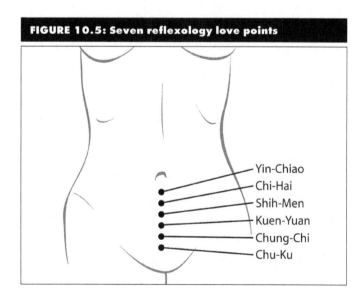

FIGURE 10.5: Seven reflexology love points

Yin-Chiao
Chi-Hai
Shih-Men
Kuen-Yuan
Chung-Chi
Chu-Ku

Before undressing your partner, slip your fingers along the edge of their boxers, undies, or panties. Sliding your fingers outward, touch the light hollow just before you reach the hipbone, in order to potentially cause a reaction.

Traveling slightly downward and outward, you will find two acupressure points located along the crease where the leg and trunk of the body join: Rushing Door and Mansion Cottage. Rushing Door is located in the middle of this crease; Mansion Cottage lies about an inch above and outward from Rushing Door (see Figure 5.2 on page 73). Stimulating these points, which act as major gates for energy flow into the genitals and throughout the reproductive system, can send a sexually arousing rush of circulation to the genitals and legs, resulting in enhanced sexual pleasure.

❧ EXERCISE 10.3: *Just the Trick*

Place the heels of your hands on the creases where your partner's thighs join the trunk. Resting your fingertips lightly on the belly, slowly lean your weight into the Rushing Door points; hold this position for a minute or two, gradually increasing the pressure. Ask your partner to breathe into your hands. With practice, you can do this during oral sex or while kissing and stimulating other erogenous zones.

The Thighs

The thighs are a hotbed of hot spots, especially because the upper thighs are so close to the genitals. Stimulating the inner thighs and the back of the upper thighs can build scintillating sexual tension. Experimenting with different caresses will not only act as a tease but will also send your lover into a sexual frenzy. Try long massages up the thigh that end with your fingertips grazing the genitals, feathery-light touches that send shivers up your partner's body, or licking the nerve-packed area where back of the thigh meets the buttocks.

Pay particular attention to the acupressure and reflexology points that lie midway between the kneecap and groin (see Figure 10.6). The first, the Sea of Blood, is located two inches above each knee, where the muscles go slightly inward (see Figure 10.6). Press this point firmly with your thumb. The Inner Thigh acupressure points are located on the inside of the upper thigh, close to the crease that joins the thigh and trunk of the body (see Figure 10.6). Lightly touching, stroking, kissing, or licking these points can help to arouse your partner, especially if he's male. These points can also be easily stimulated during oral sex, whether you're between your lover's legs or lying on top of them.

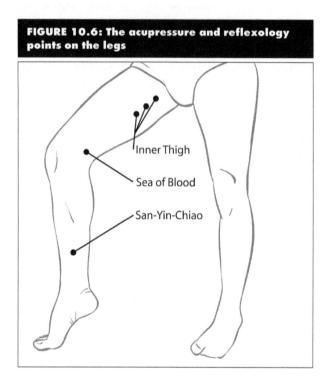

FIGURE 10.6: The acupressure and reflexology points on the legs

Inner Thigh

Sea of Blood

San-Yin-Chiao

There are twenty-one acupoints between the axillary fossa of the rib cage and femur of the thigh, and nineteen between the greater trochanter of the femur and the middle of the poplitoal crease. Becoming familiar with acupressure points and their specific health benefits can enable you to help your lover feel good in all sorts of ways. The Complete Idiot's Guide to Acupuncture and Acupressure *is a great resource for beginners (see Resources and Recommended Reading).*

The Knees

This area of the body, especially the back of the knee, is another one that is full of nerve endings, and tickling or licking it can turn your lover into putty in your hands. It's a perfect naughty spot for getting each other turned on in public. When you have a more private moment, try licking this hot spot and then blowing on it to create a warm-cold sensation.

The Shins and Calves

Your lower leg is a major hot spot because, according to sexual reflexology, it contains the most significant love point, San-Yin-Chiao, where the three yin (female sexual energy) channels intersect (see Figure 10.6). (Everyone has both yin and yang energies, so this love point exists in both women and men.) Once you find the spot, which is located on the inside of the shin, approximately three inches above the anklebone and alongside the shinbone, press this area to stimulate it. Running your fingertips over the lower leg's often-attractive shape and playing with the Achilles tendon area will woo your lover in no time.

Bodywork

Although all of the parts we have covered in this chapter can be given individual attention, sometimes we don't want to dote on just one. It's like being forced to pick a single dessert when offered a trayful—you want all of them at once! Naturally, there are times when we want to give total-body loving, focusing on all of these areas in a manner that is often more sensual than sexual.

Engaging in bodywork with your partner is one way to hit many spots without expending a great deal of effort. The yoga exercises offered throughout this book provide multispot stimulation. Many other techniques also exist that make both partners feel good. In the technique of watsu water shiatsu, for example, one partner is cradled, stretched, and slowly moved while partially submerged in water. The other partner leans the receiver's straight (but not stiff) body backward in the water. The result: Your lover can bask in the stillness of the warm water, submerged in feelings of being loved. To make this experience even more peaceful for your partner, try holding their hips or rib cage and gently swaying their body from side to side. Being careful to avoid filling your lover's nose full of water (a water pillow may help to address this concern), press the genitals or stomach. Then switch roles so you can have a turn. Many people who engage in this sort of water therapy with their lover say that it evokes a powerful emotional release, increasing trust and relaxation.

If you don't have a body of water readily available to engage in watsu water shiatsu, you can still bathe one another. This opens the blood vessels near the surface of your skin, making your body more responsive to touch, including sexual touch. During this sensuous time, take care of each other's every need, washing each other, shaving each other, shampooing each other—all the while complimenting each other's bodies and expressing what you love about your partner and your relationship. Dry each other off, wrapping your love in a soft towel or a bathrobe when finished.

Try making love while wearing a silk bathrobe, relishing its fabulous feel against your skin.

Yoga Poses for Total-Body Stimulation

◖ POSE 10.1: *Couple Cuddle (see picture on facing page)*

One lover gets into the resting pose: resting on their knees, forehead to the ground, arms extended backward at their sides. The other lover wraps themselves over the first. Now breathe together, feeling the connection, love, energy, and trust. Cuddle for at least five minutes. Switch positions. **Results:** Couples feel bonded as they exchange heat and energy and absorb the power of touch.

◖ POSE 10.2: *Tantric Embrace*

One partner lies down on their back with arms stretched upward overhead, the back of their hands on the floor. The other partner lies down on top, with their legs straddling their partner. Using the thumbs, the top

YOGA POSE 10.1: Couple Cuddle

partner stimulates the bottom partner's Spirit Gate acupressure points, which lie on the dip between the wrist bone and the center of the wrist crease (see Figure 12.2 on page 171).

Results: Fear and anxiety are relieved and harmony is strengthened in this full-body hug, a variation on tantra's Harmony Bonding pose. Partners feel each other's energy, especially through the heart chakra.

The Naughty Spots

The buttocks deserve a chapter of their own because they are a self-contained playground—plus, people love them so much! Between anal fingering, anal play, anal sex, and working the buttocks, this area of the body can really keep your hands (and face) busy.

The Buttocks

Whether or not you're into anal play, the butt itself is an amazing hot spot. Taking into account its curves, texture, size, and meatiness, it is one of the easiest erogenous zones to manipulate, whether you're spanking it during sex, grabbing and pulling it for deeper penetration during thrusting, or holding onto it just because they're your love buns. The buttocks are also one of the few intimate areas that lovers can touch while they are in public, whether slipping a hand into a lover's back pocket or giving the butt a playful slap, squeeze, or caress. Furthermore, when you're out dancing, bumping and grinding against your hottie's backside is a way of showing interest in the more advanced moves that might happen off the dance floor later in the evening.

Many lovers like to have their buttocks massaged and gripped during foreplay and sex, and this area can handle a rougher touch than other parts of the body. You can get away with more pressure here than you can elsewhere, so enjoy exerting a little more force (though only inflict pain if that's what your heartthrob desires). Some men and women like being spanked, some harder than others, with the resulting jiggling action sending a rippling effect throughout the groin. Nerve endings resonate with pleasure from the light stinging, tickling sensation as the buttocks become redder and redder. Furthermore, genital hot spots, like the scrotum and inner lips, feel the vibrating effects of butt play and ache with desire as a result.

So go ahead—grab, pinch, dig in your nails, or spank your sweetie's buttocks. During sex play, if the position allows, knead the butt cheeks firmly or tap on them gently. Run your nails along a lover's back, tickling the area where it meets the butt. Hold or grip the buttocks during sex to direct the angle, speed, and depth of penetration.

You can also play with the butt crease for a different sort of pleasure. Run your fingers or tongue up and down it, and know that lovers, especially those who are timid regarding anal sex, can derive much of the same pleasure from having their butt crease massaged as they would from full anal penetration. For **gluteal sex,** which involves one partner contracting their gluteal muscles while rotating the pelvis as the other partner thrusts a penis or dildo into the crease, lube is a *must,* unless you want a rug burn of sorts, since the crease produces no natural lubrication.

The Anus

Being the external opening of the anal canal, the anus is an area of soft tissue folds, wrinkled and puckered in appearance, which may be covered with light or dark hair. The anal area is a major hot spot when you consider that the anus and rectum are full of sensitive, responsive nerve endings. During sexual excitement, the anus and anal canal are engorged with blood, becoming even more sensitive and aroused when directly stimulated. Many couples love engaging in anal sex play, since such acts can end up stimulating a number of other erogenous zones in addition to the anus, like the G-spot and perineum in both sexes, and the prostate gland and bulb of the penis in the male. Furthermore, the rush of doing what culture deems to be forbidden can be thrilling in and of itself, with the mind getting off on the fact that you're doing something considered "dirty," "taboo," or "wrong."

Why Is the Anus Such a Hot Spot?

For some individuals, the anus is the most erogenous zone on their body and, for even more people, anal sex gives a deep feeling of sexual pleasure that is unobtainable in other ways. Some women report orgasm during anal intercourse, especially when accompanied by hand stimulation of the clitoris. Gay men also report orgasm during anal intercourse, primarily due to stimulation of the prostate—something any heterosexual male can experience as well. Having your partner wear a strap-on with a dildo can enable a man or woman of any orientation to experience the pleasures and sensations of anal sex.

Lastly, as stated in the chapter on the prostate, the forbidden nature of anal play makes it all the more desirable and sexually gratifying. This psychological component is what makes this practice highly satisfying for many lovers.

Anal Myths and Misconceptions

Myth: Anal sex play is only practiced by gay men.

Anal sex is an activity that people of all sexual orientations engage in, whether with a penis, a strap-on with a dildo, or other object. While up to 60 percent of gay men have tried anal sex, less than 30 percent have it regularly, with most opting for fellatio (oral sex). Furthermore, a number of surveys have found that 20 to 45 percent of women have engaged in anal sex. The myth and worry that anal play is a gay thing is a result of homophobia and misconceptions that say anal eroticism is only pursued by "perverts," "sluts," or "weirdos"—basically, sexual minorities.

Myth: The anal area is dirty.

Typically, there's only a small amount of fecal matter in the anal canal. Furthermore, the anus has far less exposure to germs than any external area of the body. If people have issues with cleanliness during anal play, they can opt to take a shower or bath beforehand and/or be sure to have a bowel movement or enema (an injection of liquid into the anus) to clear out the rectum.

Myth: Anal play is painful.
While at times anal sex can be uncomfortable, stressful, and painful, it does not need to be any of these things. If done in a relaxed environment with time, communication, comfort, trust between partners, and tons of lube, people can have pain-free anal sex. The anus contains a dense concentration of nerve endings. When it is relaxed and welcoming to penetration, a person will experience pleasure and even orgasm rather than pain. If you experience pain, your body is trying to tell you that something is not working. This warning should be heeded by taking a break from, or changing the process of, anal penetration.

Rules for Anal Play

❋ You need to want it. If you don't desire anal play, then it's not going to be pleasurable, and it may be downright uncomfortable, difficult, and painful. Think of trying to feed a baby when it doesn't want food. The little one's mouth clamps up and the baby throws a fit, definitely not making the feeding any easier. Your anus is likely to react in a very similar fashion if you're not up for having it stimulated.

❋ Find the right time and place that will allow you both to be relaxed and where you won't be disturbed. Anal sex is not "quickie" sex. A great deal of time needs to be devoted to getting relaxed and turned on, and to working the anal sphincter muscle to prepare it for proper, comfortable penetration. Plan for this activity at an uncrowded point in your calendar. Don't do it, for example, the night before a big test or presentation, when you might be tense and preoccupied. Anal sex requires your full effort and attention.

❋ Prepare for the event ahead of time. Have safer-sex products, lube, a towel, a washcloth, baby wipes, and anything else you need readily available. To deal with cleanliness issues, have a bowel movement and/or take an enema, especially if you are not having well-formed stools, (e.g., due to stress, diet, constipation, or diarrhea). An enema involves introduction of water or a liquid solution into the rectum to flush out the anal canal, colon, and rectum, removing fecal matter and stimulating bowels. It is a particularly good idea to have one if you're planning for a lot of anal play and for acts involving the use of larger sex toys or fisting. Showering before and after sex, and rinsing out the anus during both of these showers can also help to make the experience cleaner.

❋ Engage in lots of foreplay. Work as many hot spots as needed, especially the clitoris or penis, to get your engines revved and to allow you to loosen up and become more involved in the moment. Think about it: Professional athletes, despite being tops in their field, always warm up prior to a competition. They know that they need to do so in order to prevent injury and perform better. Translate this idea to anal sex: Even the anal-sex pros require pregame preparation and action for it to become a fulfilling, enjoyable, successful experience.

❋ Realize that with anal play, especially anal sex, proficiency will take time. You're not going to master it all at once. You might not even like it the first couple of times you try it depending on whatever issues you're grappling with or how unstimulating or disastrous the experience may prove to be if something goes wrong. Try to look at your anal-sex venture as you did learning how to ride a bike or tie your shoes. If you were like most children, you probably didn't ace it on the first try or two, but you got better and better with time and practice. Anal sex is probably going to take several attempts before both partners are comfortable with it and execute it with fluidity. Furthermore, if you're the top partner (the thrusting partner), don't give your partner a tough time about not delivering a porn star's performance; this will only squelch efforts, especially if you're unwilling to take it in the ass yourself.

❋ Consider using a latex or polyurethane condom. This will not only protect you from sexually transmitted infections like HIV, but in general it will also keep things cleaner and make things easier.

＊ Use lube—and lots of it. The rectum provides no natural lubrication and is surrounded by fairly tight muscles. It needs extra moisture for penetration to be a comfortable experience. When shopping for an anal lube, know that brands like Anal-Eze and Tushy Tamer contain an ingredient, benzocaine, that numbs the area. Don't be fooled into thinking that this effect will necessarily make things easier or more comfortable; rather, a person will simply feel fewer sensations, whether they are pleasurable or unpleasurable. This can be dangerous because pain receptivity is crucial during anal sex in order to gauge potential damage. Anal lubes worth trying include Astroglide, ID Glide, Probe Thick, Maximus, Eros Gel, and Wet Platinum. Experiment with some or all of them to find out which qualities you like best—thickness, water-based vs. silicone-based, etc.

＊ Before engaging in manual play, make sure your nails are free of jagged edges or torn cuticles, both of which can tear the rectal lining. If you have long nails, stuff a cotton ball into each fingertip of a glove to prevent poking and harming the anal lining.

＊ Relax. Relax. Relax. Breathe fully and deeply for ten to fifteen minutes, not only to calm your nerves, but also to release the stress and tension that you may be holding in your buttocks. Use this as an opportunity to get into touch with your body and to bring yourself down from everything that may have you wound up. Use visualization or meditation to calm yourself. One useful technique is to envision a positive rehearsal of the sex act. When it comes to actually getting physical, start with finger penetration, which should help to relax the anal sphincter muscle. Also, note that with first penetration, the initial sphincter muscle will start to spasm. Try to stay relaxed, breathing deeply, instead of giving into the desire to clench the anal opening.

＊ Communicate. Communicate. Communicate. This is an absolute must during anal sex! Ask your partner how she or he is doing. Ask for instruction. Give direction, saying, for example, "Slow down," "Go deeper," or "Try less." Let your partner know if something feels good or painful. Let your lover know what you want. When it comes to anal sex, silence should not be interpreted as golden.

❋ Make sure you're with a partner you can trust, and make sure that both of you trust the power dynamic. Given all of the power bestowed upon the thrusting partner, they can experience quite an unexpected head trip in feeling dominant and in complete control, especially during an act that some find more demeaning than other sex acts. If you're the top partner, make sure that you don't get carried away with your role, which can hurt your partner both emotionally and physically (due to the tearing of tissue that sometimes accompanies rough play).

❋ Stop if you feel pain. Your body tells you if it is being damaged, so listen to it.

❋ When your partner tells you to stop, don't withdraw too quickly, since this can cause damage to the rectal tissue and lining.

❋ Practice ahead of time on your own. Becoming familiar with your anal area will make it much easier to engage in such pleasures with a partner and will help you know what to expect so that you can better communicate your needs and likes. During masturbation, take the time to "warm up" your anal opening, which prepares it to accept something (which is the opposite of the activity it's used to: expelling). You can use your fingers or a sex toy and simply take your time exploring what feels good, what causes discomfort, and what works best for you (e.g., in terms of your preferred brand of lubricant).

Sexual Health Considerations

Even at its safest, anal penetration can cause minute tears in the rectal tissue, giving any virus like HIV, genital warts, chlamydia, genital herpes, hepatitis B, hepatitis C, syphilis, or gonorrhea an opportunity to spread. Using a latex condom consistently and correctly every time you have sex helps to prevent the transmission of HIV, chlamydia, hepatitis C, and gonorrhea, plus it reduces the chances of spreading genital warts, genital herpes, and syphilis. It's important to realize, however, that condoms with stimulating textures on the outside (e.g., studded or ribbed ones) may cause abrasions or irritation to the rectal tissue and may also cause discomfort to your partner. Furthermore, be careful not to use any condoms with nonoxynol-9, which can irritate the rectal lining, making it easier for HIV to get into the bloodstream. Polyurethane condoms, including the female condom, which are essentially plastic sheaths, are another option, especially if you're allergic to latex. These barrier methods are not, however, as effective as latex; the female condom has never been scientifically tested or proven for safety during anal sex.

Know that anal-oral contact puts you at risk for all of the STIs, plus hepatitis A. Using a dental dam, a condom, a glove that has been cut open into a sheet of latex, or a sheet of nonmicrowaveable Saran wrap over the anus before stimulating it with your mouth will help reduce any risk of transmission.

To reduce the chance of infection during manual stimulation, especially if you have cuts or sores on your hand, or simply to keep things cleaner, use latex gloves. For those with latex allergies, know that gloves also come in vinyl, nitrile, or neoprene.

Lastly, never insert a penis, finger, or toy into the vagina after anal sex unless a new condom is being used or the penis, finger, or toy has been washed thoroughly. Bacteria from the rectum can cause vaginitis if introduced into the vagina.

Oral Action for Anal Pleasuring

Whereas in most chapters on the various hot spots I've usually presented finger action before oral action, in the case of the anus, oral stimulation may actually be a better warm-up to help lovers become comfortable with the anus and ease into penetration play. Many people, intentionally or not, hit the anal area with their mouth and tongue when stimulating the perineum, so analingus isn't much of a stretch when considering getting into backdoor pleasures. **Analingus**, also known as rimming, is stimulation of the anus by the mouth and tongue. In performing analingus, a lover will kiss, nibble, suck, and lick the area of the anal opening, buttocks, and perineum using either an up/down or circular motion, moving along the butt crease, flicking a hardened tongue across the area, or thrusting into the anal opening with the tongue. French kissing the anal opening is another approach, during which you can also drag the inner lining of your bottom lip across the anal area for a dramatic effect.

The anus can be massaged with the tongue to stimulate the nerves of the area's muscles. Using your tongue, you can make a figure eight around your partner's anus and testicles or anus and vaginal opening. Make sure to do so slowly and purposefully.

Finger Action for Anal Pleasuring

❡ EXERCISE 11.1: *Slip Inside*

1. Get in the mood! Wine and dine each other, fool around with other hot spots, and build anticipation by knowing what's to come.

2. Massage the inner thighs, genitals, and butt cheeks. This will help to increase blood flow, making the whole area more charged and ready for sex play.

3. Using a lubricant, moisten the bottom (receiving) partner's anal opening.

4. Using a well-lubed finger, touch the opening. As the anus relaxes, slip your finger inside, just up to the first knuckle, resting for a few moments as the anus gets used to having a foreign object inside of it. (Note: Depending on how tight your partner is, you may want to start with your pinkie finger rather than a larger one.)

5. Check in with your lover to make sure that they are breathing deeply.

6. As the sphincter muscles relax, and as your partner exhales, slowly and gently slip your finger farther inside, maintaining pressure against the front rectal wall.

If your partner experiences pain at any point, try slowly withdrawing and adding more lubricant or stop penetration and simply keep the finger in place to see if the pain subsides. If size is an issue, you can try using a smaller finger or toy. If these suggestions don't work, stimulate other hot spots to take things back a step or stop entirely and simply relax together.

7. When your partner is comfortable, begin to move your finger in and out in a thrusting motion, checking with your lover about the feelings caused by the depth, speed, and pressure of your action.

You can repeat this exercise using more than one finger. In doing so, it may be easier to cross your middle finger over your index finger, an action that will provide the most direct stimulation to your partner's G-spot. As you and your partner's technique becomes more advanced, you can use more fingers or move on to the use of a slender dildo or butt plug.

❦ TIPS ❧

Build your comfort level on your own time.

Practice controlling your external sphincter. Visualize that you are holding an object, like a marble, in your anus. As you imagine sucking it in, tighten your muscles, and as you imagine pushing it down, release your muscles. As you continue to visualize, change the size of the object, perhaps to that of a ping-pong ball, imagining in detail what the object would feel like in your anal sphincter and how you could control its location. Another good idea for building your comfort with anal play is to start with smaller sex toys, like dildos and butt plugs, to get yourself warmed up and used to the idea of having something in the orifice.

Press on other hot spots while stimulating the anus.

In particular, pressing on the sacrum or perineum is sure to yield great results.

Try 69, this time stimulating each other's anuses!

Fantasize.

To help you to become comfortable with an act, let your mind take you away, especially if you have issues with anal play. Pretend, for example, that you're a porn star, known for having the most desirable backside in the entire industry, or that you are a stripper or a rock-band groupie. Let yourself feel naughty. Taking on another role may help to make it more psychologically acceptable to engage in anal play.

Stimulate the G-spot during anal play.

Double penetration is an option for women who like having both their anus and vagina stimulated at the same time. Between two lovers, this can be done with fingers in both orifices or with a finger and a toy or two toys or a penis and a toy (whether or not it's a dildo). Some women handle such stimulation with relative ease, while others need more effort, warming-up, and practice, especially if a large object is being used to penetrate the anus. A very different ball game from anal sex by itself, double penetration requires a lot of time, patience, and practice.

Anal Fisting

While it's not for everyone, some people enjoy handballing, or anal fisting, in which a partner's entire hand is gradually inserted into the anus. "Anal fisting" is a misnomer, however, because it's not a person's actual fist being inserted since the fingers aren't curled during penetration. They are, rather, straight or overlapping.

Not an amateur activity, fisting requires everything anal sex does, but a lot more of it—a lot more time, practice, relaxation, patience, desire, communication, trust, lube, and education. Cleanliness is of even greater concern since there is a much larger chance of rectal tissue tearing, and the use of a latex or nonlatex glove by the fister is a must, given the increased chance of bleeding. To learn more about how to properly, safely engage in anal fisting, check out Tristan Taormino's The Ultimate Guide to Anal Sex for Women, *2nd edition (see Resources and Recommended Reading).*

Anal Intercourse

Many lovers like anal sex because it can provide a tighter feel than other types of stimulation and is great for prostate stimulation. It is typically done with both partners face down in a rear-entry position or in a man-on-top position, though there are lots of other positions that allow for anal sex (see Chapter 14 from some examples). Doggie style is the easiest if you're the thruster, because it allows you to easily see your partner's anus and what you're doing, allows for good angle of penetration, and helps you with balance, rhythm, and thrusting.

❧ EXERCISE 11.2: *Anal Probe*

1. Start by going through steps 1–7 of the finger-penetration exercise (Exercise 11.1: Slip Inside).

2. After getting the anus warmed up with your finger(s), lubricate the penis or dildo (and condom), and gently and slowly insert the (condom-covered) penis or toy into the rectum. Keep checking in with your partner to make sure they are doing okay: "Does that feel good?" "Do you need me to slow down?" "Let me know when you want me to go farther."

3. When your partner is ready, slowly begin thrusting, keeping a controlled pelvic thrust, taking care not to tear the anal lining (or the condom).

4. Regularly ask how your partner is doing to make sure that they are comfortable and pain free.

5. Continue thrusting, speeding up the pace as much as the bottom partner can handle, being sure to communicate with them to make sure that everything is all right.

6. Either one of you can stimulate the bottom partner's genitals, nipples, or other hot spots for even more head-spinning results.

Yoga Poses for Buttocks Stimulation

❧ POSE 11.1: *Stimulation of Buttocks*

One partner's position: Get into a version of Frog Pose (Bhekasana), by lying on your stomach, legs apart, feet flexed. Your weight should be on your knees and your forearms as you lift your torso up.

YOGA POSE 11.1: Stimulation of buttocks

Other partner's position: Mimic your partner's pose, pressing your belly into their buttocks, straddling your lover from behind. Your weight should be supported by your knees and hands, and your arms should be spread straight on either side of your partner's waist.

Breathe simultaneously, holding for one to five minutes.

Results: This is a great position in which to breathe and channel energy into your root chakra, releasing sexual energy; plus, it helps your flexibility, preparing you for more advanced sexual positions. The bottom partner's rear end is stimulated as well.

❧ POSE 11.2: *Buttocks Play*

One partner's position: Get into Goddess Pose (Supta Baddha Konasana), lying flat on your back, soles of your feet together, knees apart and falling toward the floor.

Other partner's position: Facing your partner's feet, get into Upward Dog (Urdhva Muhka Svanasana). With your legs lying on either side of your lover's head, place your hands on either side of their feet and lift your upper body till your arms are straight.

Hold for up to five minutes.

YOGA POSE 11.2: Buttocks play

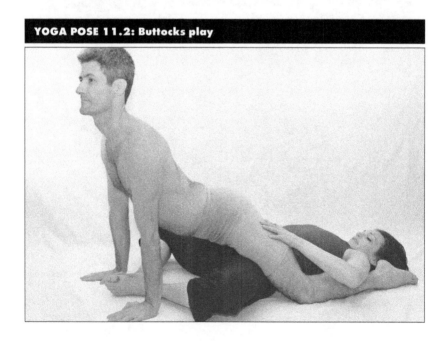

Results: This position allows the bottom partner to play with the top partner's buttocks and provides easy access to the perineum for stimulation there.

✑ POSE 11.3: *Pelvis on Buttocks Stimulation*

One partner's position: Lay on your back and lift your legs straight up in the air, maintaining your balance by keeping your hands on your lower back. Slowly bring your legs over your head, until your toes touch the floor behind your head. You may choose to bend your legs slightly or you can keep them straight. Keep your chin away from your chest, to maintain your breath, as your partner rests their pelvis against your buttocks. You can then grab the back of your lover's thighs, which allows you to stay more connected.

Other partner's position: Get on your knees behind your partner's legs. Press your hips into their buttocks as you bend backward into a partial Camel Pose (Ustrasana), your hands resting on your lover's heels, your back arched.

Hold for up to one minute.

YOGA POSE 11.3: Pelvis on buttocks stimulation

Results: The heart chakras open, allowing for more emotion, affection, and love. The hips stimulate the first partner's buttocks.

12

The Melting Spots

On a basic level, having your hands and (especially) your feet mas-saged and kneaded feels absolutely divine. On a grander scale, the practice of applying pressure to specific points on the hands and feet, typi-cally known as reflexology, is believed to influence the health of the corre-sponding body parts. Reflexology holds that pressure sensors located on the hands and feet are connected with other parts of the body, and that stimulating these sensors sends waves of relaxation throughout the body. A series of pressure techniques can be used to stimulate specific areas with the intent of invoking a beneficial response in the corresponding body part(s)—a reflexive reaction that passes throughout the nervous system.

The Hands

We put your hands to work a lot in this book, and it's no wonder that they are so heavily involved in sex play. The hands, with each palm containing forty thousand nerve endings, give and receive. Understandably, with so much power residing in the hands, massaging them can relax the entire body; furthermore, the stimulation of specific points in the hands acti-vates and balances sexual energy, as illustrated in the following diagrams (see Figure 12.1). Note the places that correspond with the body's chakras, like the solar plexus (diaphragm) and throat (thyroid/parathyroid glands). These are places to target if your aim is to get your lover's energy flowing, to activate your own energy, or to stimulate areas of the reproductive system.

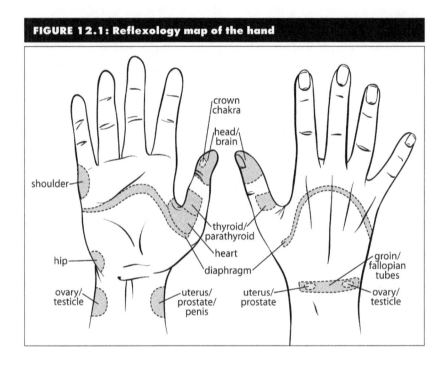

FIGURE 12.1: Reflexology map of the hand

So the next time you're toying with your honey's hand, don't overlook the erogenous effects of teasing and tickling the palm, or lightly scratching progressively bigger circles into it or tracing its lines or licking, sucking, and kissing certain areas. Be sure to massage the fingers, paying special attention to the padded area between the bottom two knuckles of each finger. Massaging the muscle between the thumb and first finger can have a stress-relieving effect. If you're holding a female's hand, dote on her pinkie finger, an area that Chinese sexology associates with the heart meridian in the belief that it houses a strong energetic connection with the emotions and sexual center. If you're playing with a man's hand, pamper his middle finger, which is associated with the circulation sex meridian, a.k.a. the heart. In either gender, the heart can be stimulated by paying particular attention to the area located below the joint where the thumb meets the rest of the hand (see Figure 12.1 on previous page).

> *Oral action on the fingers provides yet a different kind of sensual stimulation. Flicking your tongue against the palm's center or sucking on outstretched fingers always plants ideas about other ways your oral talents can be put to use. Licking foods like peanut butter or frosting from your own or your lover's fingers is always a scrumptious invitation to sex play.*

❦ EXERCISE 12.1: *The Hand Job Reinvented*

1. Decide who is to be the giver and who is to be the receiver.

2. Close your eyes and take your partner's left hand. Encourage your lover to close their eyes in order to better concentrate on the energy and sensations being cultivated in the hand.

3. Feel the hand's energy as you hold it, noting your own energy, too.

4. Breathe deeply, sending energy through your hand.

5. Explore your partner's hand—its bones, its nails, and the lines of its palm.

6. Lovingly massage it, experimenting with different pressures and strokes.

7. Check in with your partner about what feels good.

8. With your partner's palm facing downward, work your way down to the joint where the thumb meets the base of the hand. The area that runs from this point across the back of the hand to where the hand and wrist meet is a reflexology zone that stimulates the groin (see Figure 12.1). (Throughout the exercise, have your partner visualize the body part that is being stimulated.)

9. Slowly walk your thumb across this zone several times, using the thumb-walking technique described in Chapter 1 (under "Reflexology"). You can also use what is known in reflexology as the "hook-and-back-up" method, which is ideal for working a specific point.

Rest your active thumb against the area you want to massage. Bend your thumb at the first joint (the one closer to the tip). Press against the skin with the edge of your thumb and pull back with it. Pressing your four fingers into the palm adds leverage, allowing you to hook with the thumb and to pull back. Take care to avoid digging your fingernails into your lover's flesh.

10. Using your fingertip, press the area on the inner wrist (palm side) that lies about an inch inward from the base of the thumb; this will stimulate your partner's prostate or uterus.

11. Move across the wrist, using a massaging motion, until you reach a point about half an inch from the outer (pinky side) edge of the wrist. Apply the hook-and-back-up movement to this point to stimulate your partner's left ovary or testicle.

12. Repeat the process on your partner's right hand to stimulate the right side of your partner's body.

During any kind of sex play, especially as thrusting begins during intercourse, touch each other's fingertips. Activation of this supersensitive area is sure to have a dreamy effect.

❧ EXERCISE 12.2: *Palm Power*

1. Sit with your legs crossed, facing each other.

2. One partner puts their hands on their own knees, palms up.

3. The other partner places their palms face down on top of the other's hands, so that the centers of the palms touch.

4. Breathing in unison, take long, slow, deep breaths, feeling the energy that's moving between the two of you. Sense the energy moving throughout your entire body, through all of the chakras, meridians, and acupressure points.

5. Feel your and your partner's sexual energy synchronize as you inhale and exhale.

◖ **EXERCISE 12.3:** *Stimulating the Chakras*

1. Hold your partner's right thumb with your left hand.

2. Starting at the base of the thumb, slowly walk your thumb over the thyroid/parathyroid gland area several times (see Figure 12.1 on page 167), which will help to stimulate the throat chakra.

3. Move upward along your partner's thumb, making a series of walks with your own thumb to stimulate the head and brain reflex areas (the third-eye and crown chakras; see Figure 12.1).

4. Holding your partner's right hand with your left, use your right thumb to walk across the heart reflex area at the base of the thumb (see Figure 12.1), activating the heart chakra.

5. Dig your thumb into the web between your partner's thumb and index finger, and massage this area to work the chest and breast.

6. Hold your partner's fingers with your right hand, and walk your left thumb across the area on the back of the hand where the hand and wrist meet to stimulate the groin (and fallopian tube) reflex areas (see Figure 12.1), activating the sacral chakra.

7. Place your left index finger on the ovary/testicle reflex area (see Figure 12.1), and rotate your lover's hand in a clockwise motion several times.

8. Repeat the same action, only this time using a counterclockwise motion.

9. Repeat the rotating motions of steps 7 and 8 several times.

10. Use the same rotating motion, only this time place your right index finger on the uterus/prostate reflex area (see Figure 12.1) and turn your lover's hand with your left hand.

11. Repeat steps 1–10 using the other hand.

The Wrists

The wrists deserve special attention because they house two important acupressure points. Holding the Spirit Gate point, located on the dip between the center of the wrist crease and wrist bone (see Figure 12.2), balances the emotions, and stimulating a point in the center of the wrist crease increases spiritual intimacy. Either point can be held with your thumb or middle finger while grasping your partner's wrist. Holding these points after climax can reestablish your emotional balance, helping the two of you bond in heart and mind. Holding the Inner Gates point, which lies three finger-widths from the wrist crease on the center of the inside of the forearm (see Figure 12.2), helps to soothe, nurture, and rejuvenate a sexual relationship. Press this point with your thumb, holding it for a couple of minutes, as both of you breathe slowly and deeply.

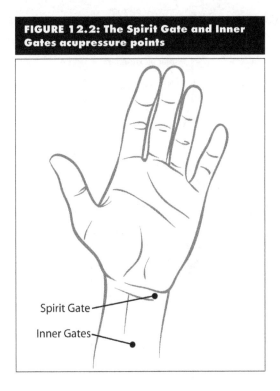

FIGURE 12.2: The Spirit Gate and Inner Gates acupressure points

Spirit Gate

Inner Gates

The Feet

Like the hands, the feet are full of pressure sensors that communicate with the brain, internal organs, and other body parts (see Figure 12.3 on the next page). As you look at the following diagrams, note the places on the foot that correspond with the groin and the chakras.

FIGURE 12.3: Reflexology map of the feet

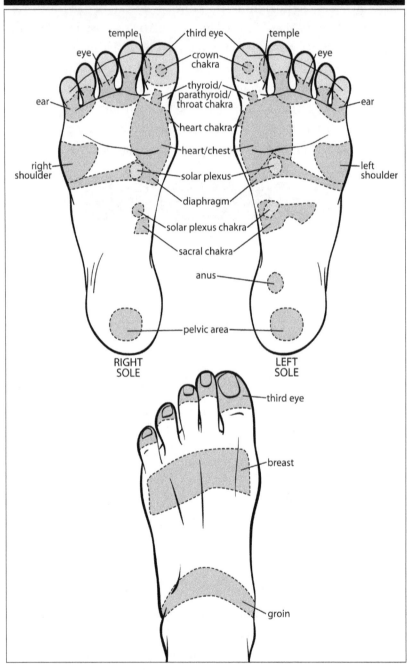

Acupressure points also abound in the foot area. The Bigger Stream point lies between the Achilles tendon and the inner anklebone (see Figure 12.4). The Bubbling Spring point lies in the center of the sole of the foot (see Figure 12.4). Using your thumbs to simultaneously press into both points on the same foot for a minute, as both of you breathe deeply, activates and stabilizes sexual energy.

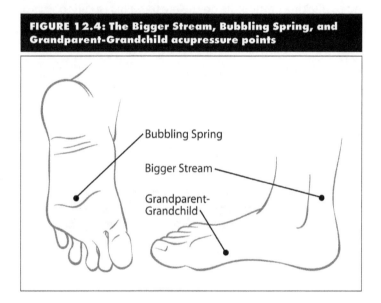

FIGURE 12.4: The Bigger Stream, Bubbling Spring, and Grandparent-Grandchild acupressure points

❁ EXERCISE 12.4: *Foot Fetish*

1. Massage each foot with a well-oiled hand for at least five minutes.

2. Put your index finger between your lover's big toe and second toe. Turn your wrist side-to-side as you lift your finger. Repeat for each space between the toes.

3. Massage the ball of the foot for about thirty seconds. This corresponds to a point on the liver meridian, which encircles the external genitalia and runs up through the breasts. It's also an important point for draining your lover's tension.

4. As your partner becomes more relaxed, stretch the arch of the foot back by flexing the ankle, and lightly lick the valley between the

second and third toes. This affects the middle of the sole, stimulating the Bubbling Spring point (referred to in reflexology as Yung-Chuan; see Figure 12.4 on the previous page).

5. Performing the same action as above about an inch below the ball of the foot stimulates the Grandparent-Grandchild acupressure point (see Figure 12.4), cultivating a sense of security in your relationship.

6. End by sucking or nibbling on the big toe. This is said to release instant sexual energy because the liver meridian, which encircles the external genitalia, originates here.

7. Give ample attention to the acupressure points Hidden Clarity and Great Sincerity, which lie, respectively, at the outer and inner corners of the big toe at the base of the nail (see Figure 12.5). These points calm the spirit and clear the brain when touched, sucked, or kissed.

8. Repeat steps 1–7 on the other foot.

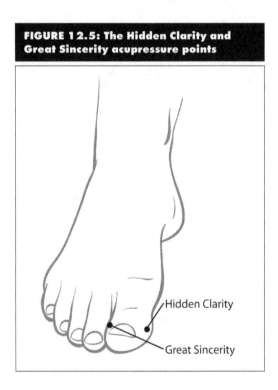

FIGURE 12.5: The Hidden Clarity and Great Sincerity acupressure points

❦ EXERCISE 12.5: *Playing Ball*

1. Cup your lover's heel in one hand, with your thumb resting on the outside of the ankle and your middle finger on the inside.

2. Using your other hand, hold the ball of the foot as you turn the foot to its right as far as it will go, maintaining constant pressure.

3. Do this a few times; then repeat the action going in the opposite direction.

4. Cup a golf ball between the palm of your hand and your lover's foot.

5. Roll it over the area, pinpointing the parts that stimulate the chakras or sex organs (see Figure 12.3 on page 172).

6. End the session by placing your thumbs at the solar-plexus reflex area of the foot, pressing lightly (see Figure 12.3). Along with your partner, take three simultaneous breaths.

❦ EXERCISE 12.6: *Stimulating the Chakras and Then Some*

1. Rest your right thumb on the thyroid-gland and parathyroid-gland reflex areas (see Figure 12.3). At the same time, use your left hand to hold the big toe in place to stimulate the throat chakra (see Figure 12.3).

2. Using the thumb-walking technique, work your right thumb from right to left across the reflex area several times.

3. Change directions, this time with your right thumb holding the big toe backward as your left thumb walks across this area.

4. Repeat a few times.

5. Hold all the toes backward with your left hand.

6. Starting at the diaphragm reflex area (see Figure 12.3), walk your right thumb up through the heart and chest reflex areas (see Figure 12.3) several times to enliven the heart chakra.

7. Move your thumb to the solar-plexus reflex area (see Figure 12.3), walking over it several times in an upward motion to stimulate the corresponding chakra.

8. Put your right index finger on the inside of your lover's left ankle-bone, and put the tip of your ring finger on the heel's back corner. Pull your middle finger inward until it is in alignment with the other two fingers. This is the uterus/prostate reflex area.

9. Place your left middle finger on this point, cupping your partner's heel in your hand.

10. Grasping the ball of the foot with your right hand, turn the foot clockwise several times, returning it to the neutral position between each turn.

11. Hold the foot with your left hand, placing your right hand on the breast reflex area (see Figure 12.3).

12. Spread the second and third toes apart, and walk your index finger down this area on the top part of the foot.

13. End the session by holding the foot with your right hand and walking your left thumb across the groin reflex area (see Figure 12.3).

14. Repeat steps 1–13 on the other foot.

13

Too Hot to Handle: Sex Toys for Fun and Pleasure

What you have read concerning the body's hot spots would not be complete without a review of some of the many sex toys out there, which are designed exclusively for your erogenous pleasuring. Before we round out the book with a discussion of all the positions that can enhance hot-spot action (see the next chapter), we need to put first things first. After all, you may find the following enhancement products useful in your boudoir pursuits.

Whether you surf a sex-toy website or walk into a shop, the experience can make you feel like a kid in a candy store. What kind of sweet are you in the mood for? They all look so good—why can't you just have a Pooh Bear smackerel of each?

Today, there are more sex toys on the market than ever, in all sorts of styles, shapes, colors, textures, and price ranges. The decision about which one, or ones, to purchase can be a heat-inducing sexual experience in and of itself, as you daydream about all the different ways a sexual enhancement can be used—and all the hot spots it can be used on.

Although the sexual enhancements discussed in this chapter are marketed as "official" eroticizers, a **sex toy** can be anything used to enhance your sexual pleasure. The ones described here are among some of the most popular available. These can be used on many hot spots, so don't be afraid to experiment. Just make sure you use them safely and properly to avoid hurting yourself or transmitting infection. See the Resources and Recommended Reading section, located at the back of the book, to find retail outlets for any of the products mentioned here.

Rules for Sex-Toy Play

❋ Do not exchange sex toys with another person unless the toys have first been properly cleaned. This helps to prevent the spread of sexually transmitted infection(s).

❋ Whether by yourself or with a partner, never use a toy anally and then vaginally without first cleaning it properly. Doing so can introduce bacteria and viruses into the vagina, leading to infection.

❋ Stick with toys that have a wide, flared base or sturdy cord, especially during anal play.

❋ Lube it up.

❋ Do not use silicone lube with a silicone sex toy. Over time, a silicone lube can cause the toy's silicone to dissolve. Using a condom over the toy will solve this problem.

❋ Make sure to clean all toys thoroughly with warm water and mild antibacterial soap after using them. Allow them to completely dry before storing them in a cool, dry, dust-free place. Proper care of your sex toys can help to prevent undesirable bacterial growth.

❋ If your sex toy is made of vinyl, covering it with a condom is highly recommended. Vinyl toys are porous, and using a condom is the only way they can be kept properly clean and remain bacteria-free. Silicone toys, plastic toys, and toys with cords (not electrical cords) can be boiled and cleaned with soap.

❋ Never substitute random objects for anal toys when engaging in anal play; some objects have been known to get stuck.

❋ When it comes to cock rings, don't use substitutes like rubber bands, which can cause permanent damage. Stick with the real thing—it's well worth the investment.

Sexual Health Considerations

As I have already mentioned, sharing a sex toy can put one at risk for STIs; namely, chlamydia, gonorrhea, hepatitis B, hepatitis C, and HIV. If a toy is made of jelly, rubber, or vinyl, all of which are porous materials that therefore cannot be disinfected, you should either only use it on yourself or cover it with a condom and change condoms when you want to change partners or orifices. If the toy is made of silicone, metal, glass, or acrylic (nonporous materials), it can be (1) disinfected before use on another partner by using hot water and an antibacterial soap or by rinsing it in a ten-to-one bleach solution (ten parts water to one part bleach), or (2) covered with a condom that is changed between partners and between use in different orifices on the same partner.

As you read about the recommended ways for using each of the following sex toys, consider where else they can be used and how. Don't limit yourself to the major hot spots discussed here. For example, your fingers and tongue do a sensational job of stimulating your erogenous zones, but using a toy on your acupressure and/or reflexology points can make for a totally different experience. Don't be afraid to think outside of the box.

Vibrators

Although these are best known for their genital pleasuring, especially clitoral, vibrators can be used almost anywhere on the body of either sex. You can work this type of motorized, handheld device, which often resembles a penis or wand, all over the body to release tension and build orgasmic response.

FIGURE 13.1: A variety of vibrators

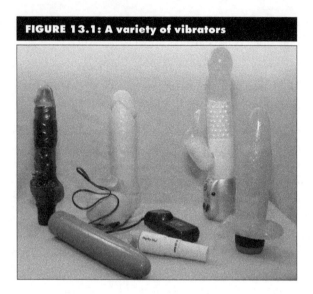

To titillate the male genitals, you can rub a vibrator up and down the penile shaft from head to base, slide it just behind the testicles, and push it firmly onto the perineum, all while carefully experimenting with different speeds. Make sure to continue using your free hand to stimulate other hot spots. The men's toy called the Pleasure Wand is a particularly enticing model because it massages the scrotum and balls while stimulating the prostate. Its four speeds offer a range of action from mild to powerful, and its handle is designed to ensure easy insertion and removal.

Women who use vibrators tend most often to focus on the clitoris. Many women report having had their first orgasm or first multiorgasmic experience while experimenting with a vibrator. This may happen the first time she uses a vibrator or after a few times of fooling around and becoming more comfortable with it, with or without a partner. It's important not to put pressure on yourself or your lover to have an earth-shattering response to this toy; any loaded expectations can shut down orgasmic response, making the whole experience more stressful than fun.

To use a vibrator on the clitoris, work it either back and forth or up and down. A circular motion will also produce rave reactions. No matter what motion you use, the trick is to ease off every now and then so the clitoris does not become numb and desensitized. Take this opportunity to move the vibrator to her inner lips, perineum, and mons pubis, sending vibrations throughout her entire vulva.

Clitoral stimulators come in a variety of shapes, sizes, colors, and textures, and they offer many different features. For example, there are silver egg-shaped vibrators, dial-controlled battery packs, and a host of waterproof, jelly, plastic, double-headed, and ribbed models. Some are remote-controlled, secured in place with straps or panties, for discreetly taking one's pleasure out in public. Some vibrating toys are meant to pleasure more than one spot. The vibrating cock ring can provide both clitoral and penile stimulation. Some varieties come with a "clitickler" attachment, a soft rubber sheath of sorts that helps the vibrator cup the clitoris, focusing sensations directly onto this spot. Among the bestsellers at my website, www.sexualitysource.com, are the Blue Waterproof Delight and the Ultra-Tech 3000, a less expensive but equally satisfying version of the infamous Rabbit vibrator.

G-spot vibrators and attachments open up a whole new world of moves and stimulation. Among the plethora of choices, the Rabbit Habit has been an international sensation. Its "rabbit ears," which can be adjusted to vibrate at different speeds, flutter against the clitoris, and the attached shaft moves to stimulate both the G-spot and the vaginal opening.

"Tongues" are vibrators that feature a flattened, tongue-shaped top that wags back and forth. Designed mostly for mimicking cunnilingus, "tongues" can be used on other hot spots, like the anus or nipples. This type of vibrator can also stimulate the entire vulval area.

As sex toys become increasingly more advanced and more expensive, don't be afraid to experiment with household products. After all, the Hitachi magic wand got its start as a home back massager, and it is now recommended as a sex toy, especially for women who have orgasmic disorders. When you first use the Hitachi, be sure to place a towel or panties between it and the clitoris because the vibrations it produces can be too strong for some women. Other household gadgets you could use for clitoral sex play include Jacuzzi jets, the other end of your electric toothbrush (made more sanitary by covering the unit with a washcloth or paper towel), or a shower massage device, which can be aimed to spray hot water directly against your clitoris.

Pumps and Cylinders

A 3-inch-tall by ⅝-inch-wide cylinder with a handheld vacuum, the clit pump is a device that temporarily expands the size of the clitoris. It does this by drawing the clitoral flesh into the tube via an intense suction, enhancing this hot spot's sensitivity using a pulling sensation. It can also be used on the nipples in a circular motion, stimulating them with vibrations and suction that cause increased blood flow. It's perfect for sadomasochistic (S&M) or gender sex play, because a woman or her lover can control the intensity and duration of the suction with a quick release of the unit's hand pump. Since the suction is very strong, be sure to carefully read the product's safety information before using it.

The Eros Clitoral Therapy Device (Eros-CTD), approved by the FDA for women with arousal disorders, enhances clitoral sensitivity and women's responsiveness. A soft suction cup is placed over the labia and clitoris, and a squeeze-bulb hand pump evacuates air from the cup, gently drawing extra blood into the clitoris in order to increase its erotic sensitivity. Women who are in need of increased blood flow to the genitals, and those who aren't, have found that the device helps to increase vaginal lubrication and clitoral sensations, provides greater sexual satisfaction, and aids them in more easily expressing orgasm, though these reactions vary from woman to woman, if any change is noticed at all. Available by prescription only, the device has no side effects.

A similar device, Selene, which is designed specifically for clitoral benefits, is available without a prescription. This pump, which may be used with or without its vibratory feature, pulls blood into the clitoral area and the surrounding tissue, powerfully stimulating the clitoris. Created by sexologist Dr. Laura Berman, the Selene is said to increase genital lubrication, sensation, and the ease of attaining orgasm.

Nipple Teasers

Nipple teasers, or clips, clamp onto the nipples to provide sensation either during breast play or during the entire interaction if left in place. They come in a wide range of sizes that allow users to adjust the pressure.

Tugging on the toy's chain or activating its vibrator attachment (if it has one) provides even more stimulation.

For those who are into strong nipple stimulation, nipple rings are a version of this toy that create arousal sensations without actually piercing the nipple. Stimulation strength is altered by pulling the clips apart, and a lover can tug them off at the height of climax to produce more body-tingling sensations.

Butt Plugs

Inserted into the rectum, a butt plug (such as the Hot Pinks Love Plug) can be used in a thrusting motion or, if it has a flare around the middle, can be left in place during other sex acts. Either way, a butt plug provides a feeling of fullness that users like, and it can heighten one's climax. Butt plugs are available in different sizes, shapes (e.g., phallic-shaped), and textures (ribbed, bumpy, ridged, or smooth); usually have a flared base (to prevent it from getting "lost" in the rectum); and sometimes come with a vibrator feature (which can help to relax the anal muscles). Note: This type of toy may slip or shoot out of the anus as you become aroused or climax.

Climax Beads

Ranging from soft to firm in texture, climax, or anal, beads usually consist of four to ten balls made of latex or hard plastic that are strung along a length of plastic, rubber, cotton, or nylon cord, often with a ring at the end. Available in a variety of sizes, with half-inch-diameter balls being the most popular, the entire string of beads is inserted into the anus, one lube-coated bead at a time, stimulating anal nerve endings and providing prostate massage. This experience can be made even more pleasurable if it is accompanied by the stimulation of other hot spots. The beads are typically left in place until the user is near climax, when they are pulled out, slowly and gently, one by one, intensifying orgasm. Using a condom over the beads, with a knot tied in the end of the condom, helps to keep them clean (especially since the soft or jelly rubber beads are difficult to clean).

Ben wa balls are a different type of climax bead, meant more for vaginal play. These solid-metal balls can be used in much the same way as anal climax beads.

Skin Stimulants

Human skin craves touch and sensation, and many objects can be used to create different tactile sensations in order to satisfy that desire. A feather (for example, a foot-long ostrich feather) can tickle the skin, teasing areas from the armpits to the treasure trail. Body paints provide slippery sliding action, and partners can draw hearts, write sweet nothings, and sketch erotica onto each other's bodies. These paints come in flavors like cherry, mint, chocolate, and blueberry, so lovers can lick their masterpieces off of each other at any time during the experience.

Tassels, floggers, and whips provide unique sensations. These toys can be slapped against a person's buttocks, back, or foot—pretty much anywhere the recipient can handle it. Be sure to check in with your partner about how hard or soft they want to be stimulated. Remember, the larger the surface area of skin, the less damage (skin breakage) that can potentially occur. Materials like cowhide or rubber are harsher than horsehair or silk. Toys that employ a solid knot to keep the tail together are safer to use than those that are not bound.

The Kegelcisor

A vaginal barbell, the surgical-steel Kegelcisor is designed as a resistive device for practicing pelvic-floor exercises. It has three spheres of varying diameters; a user builds muscle tone by squeezing her PC muscle around increasingly smaller spheres. Depending on its weight and size, this device can provide G-spot pressure. A woman simply hooks it over her pubic bone and jiggles it against the G-spot area.

Genital Rings

Also known as a cock ring, a genital ring is a metal or latex object that fits over the base of the penis or around the entire penis and scrotum (note:

never use any homemade imitations, which can cause damage). Available in Velcro models or with leather snaps, the device supposedly stimulates the penis by partially "trapping" penile blood flow during arousal. For this reason, it is known to help maintain erection.

Artificial Vaginas/Mouths/Erection Sleeves

Artificial vaginas, also described as mouths or erection sleeves, are cylinders of soft rubber or plastic often designed to resemble vaginal or oral lips. A user can slide his penis between the lips into an internal pocket to simulate the feeling of intercourse, especially for the head of the penis. Vibrating models provide even more sensation.

Dildos

Made of rubber, silicone, or latex, a dildo is an artificial erect penis that can be inserted into the vagina, mouth, or anus. Dildos come in a variety of sizes, colors, textures, and styles, allowing users to choose the length, thickness, hardness, and texture that's best for them. Used for male or female G-spot stimulation, the clear, S-shaped crystal wand allows for a firm grip with maximum leverage.

Most often used to simulate penile thrusting, dildos can be worn strapped into a harness by slipping them through a hole (note: They will be about one-half inch shorter once in the harness). Harnesses typically come in two models: those with an adjustable center strap running between the legs and those with a leg strap encircling the thigh. They can be made of vinyl, leather, denim, nylon, or webbing. The two-strapped harness with a triangle front is worn like a male's jockstrap, giving the user a great deal of control, while leaving the vulva and anus accessible for stimulation. A vibrating cock ring or pearl can be slipped between the top partner's body and the harness for clitoral or penile stimulation. A strap-on dildo can be used for anal penetration (in both sexes) and vaginal penetration; a man wearing a strap-on can penetrate a female's vagina and anus at the same time. Double-shafted dildos and harnesses allow for simultaneous stimulation.

The Aneros

The Aneros is a G-spot (prostate) stimulator for men that offers more focused pressure than a dildo or vibrator. Made of nonporous material, it has small plastic wings and curved handles at the base that press against the prostate from both the inside and the outside, providing instant feedback when a man contracts his anal sphincters. This means it applies pressure to the prostate during PC exercises.

Communicating with Your Partner about Sex Toys

In responding to my first book, *The Hot Guide to Safer Sex*, young adults almost always mentioned how empowering the sex toy chapter was for them—both how much fun it had been to read with their lover and how it had inspired them to visit sex-toy shops together. They reported it made it seem okay to use sex toys, opening readers up to a whole new world of safer sex play and satisfaction.

Learning about and shopping for sex toys together can be a true bonding experience for a couple. After all, you're doing something to enhance your sex life, so the benefits are mutual! Introducing the experience as such will make your mission easier. You can say, "I love our sex life, but do you feel like going on a little adventure? I've heard the _____ is out of this world."

If you already own sex toys, try to give your lover a heads-up before whipping one out, and preferably wait till after you've learned about your lover's likes and dislikes. I remember hearing about a woman in New York City who was having a great love affair with a man until she suddenly brought out an anal toy during sex. He obliged her, almost afraid not to, but he pretty much never got in touch with her again. One can't say if it was her, the way she introduced the toy, his cultural background, the toy itself, or issues he might have had with anal play. The point is you're going to have a much better reaction if you can discuss preferences and desires for experimentation ahead of time rather than springing a toy on your lover during the act itself.

Lastly, if you can, experiment with a new toy on your own ahead of time. That way, you can be ready to explain how to use it, demonstrate how to use it, and tell your lover what you like or dislike about it. Being empowered and educated about a toy will make you sexy and desirable, helping to debunk any concerns a lover might have and making them want to join you on this sexual exploration.

14

Feel the Heat: Sexual Positions for Maximum Hot-Spot Action

Nearly all of the sexual positions described in this chapter can provide hours of heart-pumping fun for people of any sexual orientation. I've tried to be as inclusive as possible, using terms like "bottom partner" and "top partner" or "thrusting partner" and "receiving partner," so that everybody can see himself or herself engaging in these positions, whether performing vaginal-penile or anal intercourse (though anal intercourse will not be as easily performed in some positions). Also, know that when I use the word "penis," it is meant to be synonymous with "dildo." Finally, note that any time I refer to the breasts or nipples, it can apply to both genders.

Sexual Health Considerations

To prevent pregnancy and the spread of STIs during intercourse of any type, try out different condoms—various sizes, brands, and textures—to find out what works best for you and your partner. If you're allergic to latex or want more heat sensation, polyurethane condoms, like Durex's Avanti, are an option. Lambskin condoms are also available, though they're not recommended for STI prevention since they are too porous to block viruses like HIV.

When it comes to lubrication, even if a condom is lubricated, you will usually need to add more. Spermicidal condoms should be used only if you're worried about preventing pregnancy. They are not recommended for STI prevention since spermicides like nonoxynol-9 can cause minute abrasions in the vaginal or anal lining, actually increasing the risk of infection.

Water-based lubes that cause a warming sensation, like Astroglide Warming Liquid and K-Y Warming UltraGel, can heat things up a tad, though some users find that these lubes do nothing for them. At the other end of the spectrum, some users find these lubes too intense. The active ingredient, usually honey or menthol, may cause mild burning, which can lead to irritation, thus increasing the chances of infection transmission.

Missionary-Style Positions

There are many variations on the classic missionary position that can provide different kinds of hot-spot stimulation, depending on what you're after. Practically all of them allow for the thrusting partner to stimulate and caress other parts of the receiver's body and to easily control thrusting. Both partners can also usually look at each other, gaze into each other's eyes, kiss, and communicate their wanton desires. In addition, the bottom partner's Crooked Bone and Transverse Bone points (see Figure 2.1 on page 29), as well as the Inner Thigh points on both partners (see Figure 7.1 on page 97), can be stimulated in this position, releasing even more sexual energy. The top partner can hold the bottom partner's Rushing Door and Mansion Cottage points (see Figure 5.2 on page 73), increasing genital sensations. The bottom partner can press into the Womb and Vitals, Sea of Vitality, or sacral points (see Figures 2.1, 10.2, and 10.3 on pages 29, 142, and 143, respectively) on the top partner's back and buttocks. This will bring the pelvises closer, providing stronger stimulation and greater pleasure during missionary-position sex.

Contrary to popular belief, many women can experience orgasm from the missionary position. For some, this occurs because the thrusting of the penis during intercourse indirectly stimulates the clitoris by moving the vagina's inner lips, in turn causing the clitoral hood to rub back and forth across the clitoral glans. For other women, clitoral stimulation before thrusting has left their knob throbbing with sensations that are heightened even further with missionary-style sex. Still other women need continued stimulation of their clitoris for orgasm during missionary, which some skillful lovers are able to provide by slipping a hand or vibrator between her legs while thrusting into the vagina and balancing on one arm.

The CAT, or coital alignment technique, is a super adaptation of the missionary that allows for more clitoral stimulation. Women who don't normally reach orgasm during missionary may do so during CAT. Instead of the penetrating partner lying directly on top of the woman, chest to chest, with the thrusting movement occurring in and out horizontally, the top lover shifts forward and to one side so that their chest is closer to one of her shoulders. This alignment allows for the clitoris to be contacted more directly, and lovers can still enjoy each other's breasts, shoulders, necks, heads, hips, and butts.

Another way to stimulate the clitoris in this cozy position is for the woman to slowly and carefully squeeze her legs straight together between her lover's legs while her partner is inside of her (see Figure 14.1). Pressing the bottom of one foot against the top of the other will make for an even tighter fit. This is a great position if the top partner is well-endowed because thrusting won't go too deep, yet the friction in the vagina will become more intense and pleasurable as the vagina tightens. The slower thrust also enables her to feel the penis in a whole new way.

FIGURE 14.1: Missionary-style—variation #1

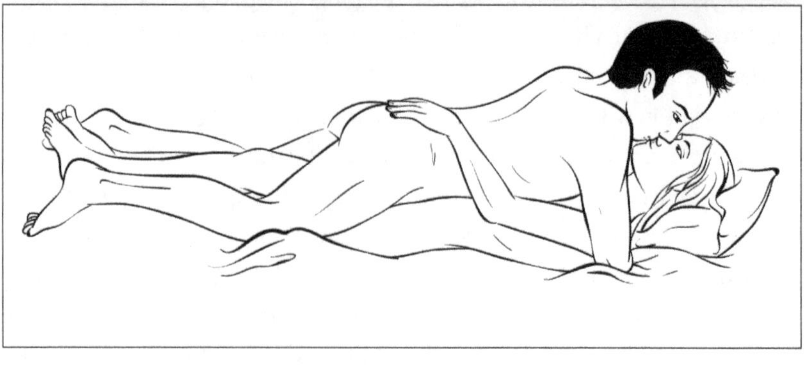

Stretching one leg out over her partner's thigh is a version of mission-ary-style sex known as "half-pressed union." This position makes for in-creased contact between her lover's body and her clitoris. The position also allows her to create more sensations during sex, as she moves her leg up and down at different angles.

Men can also enjoy this position by having their perineum stimulated by having the bottom partner reach between his legs during thrusting. Es-pecially as he climaxes, his partner can use a knuckle to gently press into this area, helping him to last longer and providing more sensation.

The top partner can sit on their knees while the bottom partner's but-tocks rest on the top partner's thighs. This allows the top partner to more easily fondle and kiss the bottom partner's entire upper body, scooping their arms under the bottom partner's back, caressing it, and pulling the torso closer. To change this position, the top partner can lean back or sit up on their knees and lift the bottom partner's pelvis during thrusting.

FIGURE 14.2: Missionary-style—variation #2

For deeper penetration, which can put pressure on the cervix, the bot-tom partner can tuck her knees into the top partner's armpits (see Figure 14.2) put her legs over the top partner's shoulders (see Figure 14.3 on the next page), or pull her knees up to her chest, toes pointing down or

FIGURE 14.3: Missionary-style—variation #3

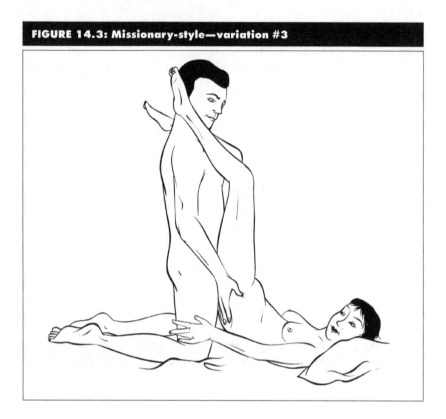

straight up in the air (see Figure 14.4). The bottom partner can grab and spank the thruster's butt cheeks, controlling the pace and depth of penetration a little bit more. Other variations include bringing her legs together and straightening them so that they're parallel with those of the top partner. (Note: Partners will not be able to see each other's faces). The thruster can then grab the bottom partner's butt. The bottom partner can also put her right leg over the top partner's left shoulder to afford a different angle during thrusting and easier belly-button and waist play (see Figure 14.5). These last two positions offer lots of opportunities for play along the back of the knee, the leg, and the ankle.

If the top partner wants to see more of their partner's buttocks, slide them to the edge of the bed and prop the receiver's legs on the top partner's shoulders. The top partner can slide their hands under the bottom partner's butt. If strong enough, the top partner can attempt to pick up the bottom partner for some unexpected fun during thrusting.

FIGURE 14.4: Missionary-style—variation #4

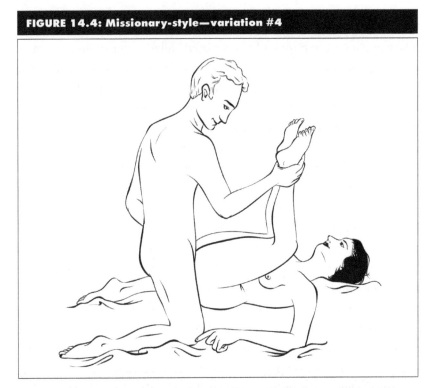

FIGURE 14.5: Missionary-style—variation #5

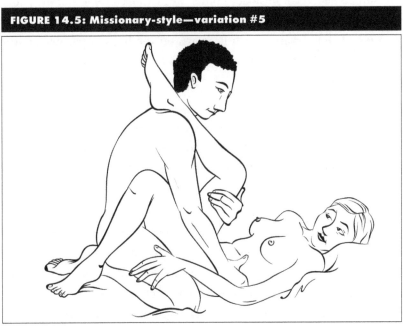

Woman-on-Top Positions

The woman-on-top position has long been hailed as one of the best for female orgasm since the woman can control her own movements, allowing her to stimulate her clitoris against her partner's abdomen. This position is most popularly portrayed with the woman sitting upright on top of her partner, with most of her weight on her knees. For deeper penetration, her partner can grab her buttocks, spreading the cheeks.

(Although this position is often referred to as "woman on top," a male partner can be the top partner for anal sex in these positions.)

A major bonus of this position is that the woman's partner can also play with her clitoris, using fingers or sex toys as she rides atop. Holding their hands up, the bottom partner can provide stimulation to the top partner's breasts during thrusting. Other parts of her body are much more accessible—and visual—to her partner as well. Furthermore, leaning back as she's riding her partner may trigger enhanced G-spot stimulation, causing sensations to radiate throughout her body. She can lean forward and stimulate acupressure points on her partner's chest (e.g., Elegant Mansion; see Figure 10.1 on page 138). If she leans back, her lover can apply pressure to her Sea of Intimacy points. The Crooked Bone and the Transverse Bone points (see Figure 5.3 on page 80) can also be activated in this position. The top partner can lie down on the bottom partner's entire body, gradually thrusting their pelvis into the bottom partner's pelvis to stimulate these points.

The clitoris's only known function is to accumulate sexual sensations and erotic pleasure! It holds a greater concentration of touch-sensitive nerve endings than any other structure in the body, including the head of the male's penis.

Other variations on this position include having the woman lie more horizontally on top of her partner, bringing her legs inside her lover's (see Figure 14.6). This results in more friction between the partners' pelvises and a snugger genital fit. She can also lean back onto her partner's thighs, leaving her clitoris even more exposed for stimulation (see Figure 14.7), or

FIGURE 14.6: Woman-on-top—variation #1

she can turn around and face the opposite way (see Figure 14.8 on the next page), which gives her more space for stimulating her own clitoris and/or her lover's testicles or vulva. If working with a penis, firmly cup his testicles and gently pull on them to the rhythm of your thrusting. With the close-up rear view afforded by this variation, her partner can play with her butt at the same time.

FIGURE 14.7: Woman-on-top—variation #2

FIGURE 14.8: Woman-on-top—variation #3

For enhanced upper-body intimacy and touch, the partner being rid-
den can sit up as the top partner leans back, supporting her weight on the
bottom partner's legs. This variation allows for great upper-body and clitoral stimulation by either partner or both at the same time yet significantly slows down the pace of thrusting. For breast and upper-body stimulation, however, the top partner should lean back onto the bottom partner
fully or prop themselves up a bit by extending their hands to the ground
(see Figure 14.9).

For great G-spot stimulation, the top partner can lie flat, face down,
and put her left leg between the bottom partner's legs while bending and
pulling up the right leg. Their legs can also be alternated. This position
also allows for more breast play.

Yet another variation involves having the top partner lean forward,
legs still bent, with her forearms placed beside her bottom partner's shoulders so that their chests are parallel. She can then pivot her hips to and fro
so that her clitoris is stimulated by the base of the penis.

FIGURE 14.9: Woman-on-top—variation #4

While certain acupressure points are recommended for stimulation with each position, I encourage you to experiment with others that I haven't mentioned. There are tons to choose from!

Side-by-Side Positions

Whether or not penetration is involved, the side-by-side position is great because it allows for clitoral or penile play when both partners face the same way and the receiving partner leans back onto the body of the other. This is a terrific position for those times when a couple wants to cuddle, relax, and engage in a lot of total-body contact and caressing, focusing especially on the neck and breasts. It is also a position that allows the body to draw sexual energy to the brain during resting periods. Sexual reflexology teaches that with partners' arms wrapped around each other, one partner can touch or massage the other's sacral points (see Figure 10.3 on page 143), activating the sacral pump and creating a sexier mouth and eyes. Also, touching or massaging the back of the heart area or the wing point of the shoulder blades is believed to increase penis hardness or vaginal wetness. Placing a hand on the sacral and crown points can make for an even greater orgasmic experience, improving erection strength and vaginal wetness. Simultaneously activating the sacral and neck points improves blood flow to sexual organs, activating the sacral and cranial pumps.

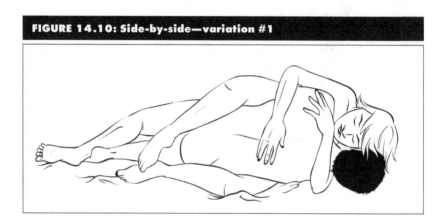

FIGURE 14.10: Side-by-side—variation #1

An alternative to this position is for partners to rest on their sides, facing each other, with one lover's legs wrapped around the other's waist (see Figure 14.10). For women, this position provides a constant friction against the clitoris as the couple rocks back and forth. Another side-by-side variation that allows for great clitoral stimulation involves the thrusting partner lying on their side while the woman's legs are thrown over the thruster's hips (see Figure 14.11). She can visually turn her lover on by playing with any part of her own body.

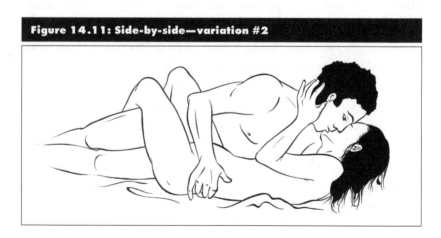

Figure 14.11: Side-by-side—variation #2

Yet another version of the side-by-side position requires the receiving partner to be on their side, facing away, knees bent and legs pulled up. The thruster's left leg is under the receiver's, and the right leg is extended straight, along the receiver's back. The thrusting partner can see the receiver's butt, as well as view the penis moving in and out of the vagina or anus.

Rear-Entry Positions

Also known as "doggie style," the rear-entry position allows a woman or her partner to reach around the front of her body to play with her clitoris, or a man and his partner to do the same with his penis and testicles, using either a hand or vibrator. Another hot spot that benefits from this position is the testicles, which can be massaged against the bottom partner; plus, the position causes the thrusting to make an erotic slapping sound against the derrière. The bottom partner's nipples can be stimulated against the sheets or pillows, especially if they are on their forearms. The Womb and Vitals and Sea of Vitality points (see Figures 2.1 and 10.2 on pages 29 and 142, respectively) on the bottom partner's backside are also easily manipulated in this position.

If partners aren't up for being on all fours, rear entry can be achieved in other ways. The bottom partner lies on their side, both knees bent in toward the chest, while the thruster positions themself behind the bottom partner, with one leg extended behind the bottom partner's back and the other between the bottom partner's legs. The bottom partner can also lie flat on their stomach, with the thruster kneeling between the bottom partner's legs, holding the buttocks for deeper penetration. If a woman puts her legs together while lying flat on her stomach, she will experience more inner- and outer-lip stimulation during thrusting.

While traditional rear entry is known to provide deep G-spot stimulation, especially if the penis is curved, as well as cervical or prostate stimulation, yet another way to hit these targets is for the bottom partner's legs to be bent and pulled up toward chest, with the top partner sitting on the penis and facing away. Keep in mind that the shallower thrusting in this position sometimes triggers a woman's G-spot more than deep thrusting does. Other versions of this position include having the bottom partner lean forward so that their head rests on one arm, propped up on a pillow (see Figure 14.12). This allows the bottom partner to reach around and play with their partner's genitals. The bottom partner can circle the base of the penis with their index finger and thumb as the top partner thrusts, providing more friction and pleasure.

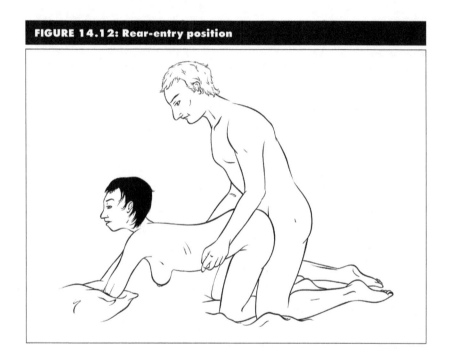

FIGURE 14.12: Rear-entry position

Sitting and Squatting Positions

In addition to slowing down thrusting movements, sitting positions can help lovers to feel closer, allow for more body contact, and help to slow down the sexual experience altogether. Acupressure points all over the body, like the neck, shoulders, and lower back, can easily be stimulated in variations of this position, taking sex to a completely different level.

When both partners sit and face the same way, the bottom partner can reach around and stimulate the top partner's clitoris or penis, or the top partner can do this to themself. The Crooked Bone, Transverse Bone, and St. 30 points (Figure 5.3 on page 80), which are located on the pelvis, can be pressed. An alternative to this position involves the receiver getting on all fours and crouching while the top partner thrusts from a position on their knees.

If the lovers face each other, the bottom partner can be on their knees, while the top partner supports their weight with their hands on the bottom partner's shoulders or knees (see Figure 14.13). An alternative to this position involves the top partner raising their legs above the bottom partner's shoulders.

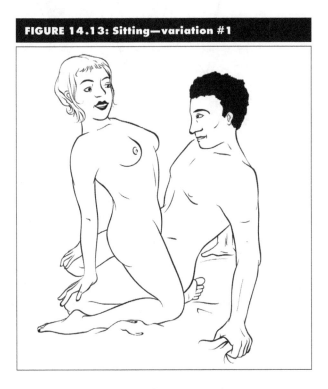

FIGURE 14.13: Sitting—variation #1

A woman's P-spot (perineum) can be stretched while both partners are sitting upright with legs wrapped around each other. Keeping the pelvises close together, the woman should arch her back, supporting her weight with one hand behind her back (see Figure 14.14 on the next page). This allows the genitals to grind together as the perineum lengthens.

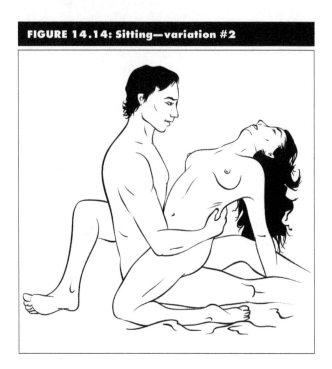

FIGURE 14.14: Sitting—variation #2

Both partners can be in a "crab" position (i.e., leaning back with their weight on their hands and feet and their buttocks 8–12 inches in the air) during thrusting, or the bottom partner can be in the "crab" position while the top partner sits on their groin, facing away.

Yet another variation is for the thrusting partner to be lying on their back, resting heels on the top partner's shoulder blades, as both partners face the same way. The top partner then controls the pace. The bottom partner can also wrap their legs around the top partner's torso if they want a tighter fit.

Standing Positions

Although it's not as leisurely as sex while sitting or lying down, on occasion, many lovers enjoy standing sex as a change of pace or because it's the only position space will allow for! Standing and facing the same way allows for clitoral or penile stimulation. Facing each other allows partners to grab each other's butts. Breasts can be stimulated in either variation.

One partner, typically the more powerful of the two, can hold the other during the standing position. This is made easier when the one being held wraps their legs around the standing lover's waist (see Figure 14.15).

FIGURE 14.15: Standing—variation #1

Alternative versions of the standing position include having both lovers kneel and face the same way (see Figure 14.16 on the next page), or face each other, with one leg of the receiving partner bent, with or without the thrusting partner's bent leg underneath it (see Figure 14.17 on the next page).

FIGURE 14.16: Kneeling—variation #1

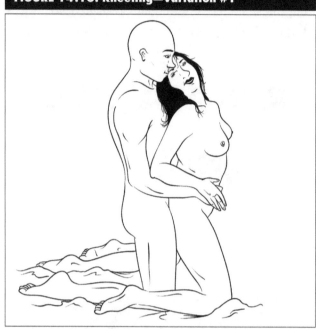

FIGURE 14.17: Kneeling—variation #2

Conclusion

My hope in writing this book has been to give people the tools they need to have more amazing sex with themselves and with their partners by utilizing some of the hottest spots on their bodies. People crave better sex and increased intimacy, and they will go to extremes to find it, often without realizing that some of the greatest sensations, feelings, and climactic peaks lie much closer to home. All they have to do is look within themselves and within their relationship and take a chance on rethinking what it means to be intimate, erotic, and connected.

Having read this book, you're well on your way to touching yourself and your lover in a more holistic, cosmically orgasmic way—physically, emotionally, and spiritually. I hope that you will use what you've learned here to rediscover yourself and your sex life. I hope that you will use it to nurture the love, lust, and trust you have in yourself and your lover. I hope that you will use it to discover sexual intimacy, blissful abandonment, and worldly rapture as you've never known them before.

Glossary

acupoints—in traditional Chinese medicine, entry points on the body's surface to the many meridians (pathways) traveling throughout the body

acupressure—the application of pressure, typically with thumbs or fingertips, to specific acupoints for therapeutic effects, e.g., relief of tension

anal fisting—(a.k.a. "handballing") a sexual activity involving gradual insertion of a partner's entire hand into another's anus

anal intercourse—a sexual activity involving the penetration of a partner's anus with a penis or dildo

analingus—stimulation of a partner's anus with one's mouth

anterior fornix erogenous zone—*see* A-spot

anus—the rectal opening located between the buttocks

aphrodisiac—a food, drink, drug, scent, or device that is believed to arouse or increase sexual desire, libido, or attraction

areola—the circular area of darker skin that surrounds the nipple of the breast

artificial vagina—*see* erection sleeve

A-spot—the smooth area located on the anterior (front) wall of a woman's vagina midway between the cervix and G-spot, which appears as a spongy, wrinkled, scrotal-like swelling and that is extremely sensitive to stimulating touch; a.k.a. "anterior fornix erogenous zone"

barrier method—a contraceptive designed to block sperm from entering the uterus, e.g., diaphragm, condom

birth control—devices or techniques used to prevent the union of sperm and egg(s) in order to avoid pregnancy; a.k.a. "contraception"

blended orgasm—in females, a climax due to simultaneous stimulation of the G-spot and clitoris; in males, a climax due to simultaneous stimulation of the prostate and penis

breasts—for females, the secondary sex organs located on the chest, composed of fatty and fibrous tissue and housing fifteen to twenty clusters of mammary glands; for males, another term for chest

butt plug—a dildo specially designed for providing anal and rectal pleasure via insertion into the anus

cervical orgasm—a climax due to stimulation of the cervix

cervix—the opening to the lower part of the uterus that protrudes into the vagina

chakra—Sanskrit word meaning "wheel," "disc," or "hub"; used to describe the seven major and minor centers of psychic energy located throughout the body

chi—(sometimes spelled "ki" or "qi") life energy

chlamydia—a bacterial sexually transmitted infection; symptoms include painful urination and/or genital discharge

climax—orgasm

clitoral hood—a sheath of tissue that protects the clitoris and is an extension of the inner vaginal lips (labia minora), which run alongside the vaginal opening

clitoral orgasm—a climax attained through stimulation of the clitoris

clitoris—on the female, a highly sensitive sexual organ located in front of the vaginal entrance and urethra that is filled with a large number of nerve endings

cock ring—a rubber, metal, or leather band worn around the base of the penis or around the entire penis and scrotum for sex play

coitus—insertion of the penis into the vagina; sexual intercourse

condom—a disposable latex, polyurethane, or sheepskin sheath placed over an erect penis that acts as a barrier to prevent pregnancy and the spread of STIs and HIV

corona—the raised ridge separating the glans (head) of the penis from the body of the penis; for many, it is the most sexually excitable region of the penis

coronal ridge—*see* corona

cunnilingus—stimulation of the female genitals with the mouth

dental dam—a latex or nonmicrowavable plastic-wrap barrier placed over the vagina or anus during sexual activity to prevent the spread of STIs

dildo—a sex toy made of rubber, silicone, or latex that can be inserted into the vagina or anus

ejaculation—the sudden, forceful discharge of semen out of the penis

erection—an enlargement of the penis that occurs when blood flows to the area

erection sleeve—a cylinder of soft rubber or plastic used to simulate the sensations of intercourse; often designed to resemble vaginal or oral lips

erogenous zone—an area of the body that is particularly sensitive to sexual stimulation

extragenital orgasm—*see* spontaneous orgasm

fellatio—stimulation of a partner's penis with one's mouth; also used to describe oral play with a dildo

female condom—a disposable, polyurethane contraceptive tube with a plastic ring at each end that is inserted into the vagina to prevent pregnancy and the transmission of STIs and HIV

female ejaculation—the phenomenon of prostatic-like fluid being expelled during G-spot stimulation and/or orgasm

fisting—a sexual activity in which a partner gradually inserts their entire hand into another's vagina

foreplay—sexual stimulation that takes place before intercourse

foreskin—in uncircumcised males, the layer of skin covering the glans (head of the penis) that retracts when the male is aroused and erect

frenulum—the tiny band of skin near the indentation on the underside of penis where the glans meets the shaft

F-spot—*see* frenulum

genital ring—*see* cock ring

genital warts—*see* human papilloma virus

genitals—the sexual or reproductive organs

glans—in the male, the smooth, extremely sensitive tip (head) of the penis that contains numerous nerve endings; in the female, the extremely sensitive, visible, external tip of the clitoris that protrudes like a small lump

gluteal sex—sexual activity involving one partner thrusting into the crease of their partner's buttocks using a penis, a dildo, or their hand/fingers

gonorrhea—a bacterial sexually transmitted infection with symptoms that include vaginal discharge, burning urination, fever, and pelvic-area pain

Gräfenberg spot—*see* G-spot

groin—the area where the thigh joins the abdomen

G-spot—in females, a small mass of erectile nerve tissue, ducts, glands, and blood vessels located on the front wall of the vagina midway between the pubic bone and the cervix; responds to sexual stimulation

hepatitis—a viral infection that can be sexually transmitted; involves inflammation of the liver and sometimes permanent liver damage and has several different strains

herpes—a viral sexually transmitted infection with two strains: herpes simplex type-1 (oral herpes) and herpes simplex type-2 (genital herpes), both of which cause blisters or sores on the given area

HIV—*see* human immunodeficiency virus

holistic practices—health activities that address the whole person; that is, mind, body, and soul

human immunodeficiency virus (HIV)—the retrovirus that causes AIDS

human papilloma virus (HPV)—a viral sexually transmitted infection that can produce warts on the genitals; a.k.a. "genital warts"

inner lips—*see* labia minora

intercourse—*see* sexual intercourse

Kabazzah—an Eastern sexual skill, often a part of Tantric practice, wherein a woman mounts a man and then moves only her internal vaginal muscles to bring him to climax while he does nothing more than stay relaxed

Kegel exercises—contractions performed to strengthen the PC muscles surrounding the genitals

Kegelcisor—a surgical-steel resistive device for practicing pelvic-floor exercises; a user builds muscle tone by inserting it into her vagina and squeezing her PC muscle around it; a.k.a. "vaginal barbell"

Kivin Method—an oral sex move in which the female's partner applies pressure to her perineum during oral sex

labia majora—the rounded pads of fatty and fibrous tissue, covered with pubic hair, that lie on either side of the vaginal entrance; the outer lips of the vulva

labia minora—the thin folds of skin that lie on either side of the vaginal entrance and extend forward to come together in front of the clitoris to form the clitoral hood; the inner lips of the vulva

male G-spot—the prostate

masturbation—self-stimulation of the genitals with the hand or an object

meridians—in traditional Chinese medicine, channels running through the body that keep the skin, muscles, organs, and psyche healthy and in balance by transporting life energy or chi

mons pubis—the fatty pad of tissue and skin lying over a woman's pubic bone that is thought to protect her pubic bone during vigorous sexual thrusting

mons veneris—*see* mons pubis

M-spot—an erogenous zone located in the vagina just below the mouth of the uterus; it can be felt when, after orgasm, the vagina lifts up, forming a "roof" or "tent" of sorts

multiple orgasms—a series of orgasmic responses that occur in succession without the person's arousal level dropping below the plateau phase

nadis—invisible channels that connect the chakras

nipple—the pigmented tip of the breast; contains erectile tissue that may provide sexual pleasure when stimulated

nipple-induced orgasm—a climax due to stimulation of one's nipple(s)

nocturnal orgasm—an involuntary orgasm that occurs during sleep; in males, most often accompanied by emission (wet dream)

oral sex—a sexual activity involving stimulation of the genitals by a partner's mouth

orgasm—a series of involuntary muscular contractions that typically peak during the third and shortest phase of the sexual response cycle and are accompanied by feelings of intense pleasure; though focused in the genitals, the contractions and sensations may spread throughout the body

outer lips—*see* labia majora

PC muscle—*see* pubococcygeus muscle

penis—the male reproductive and sex organ that passes sperm into the vagina and urine out of the body

penis-induced orgasm—a climax attained through stimulation of the penis

perineum—the soft, hairless tissue located between the genitals and anus in both sexes; a.k.a. "P-spot"

polyurethane condom—a plastic barrier worn over an erect penis that prevents pregnancy and the spread of STDs

posterior fornix zone—the erogenous area located opposite the AFE zone, on the back wall of the vaginal canal

Posterior Summit—an acupressure point located on the scalp

prana—life force; breath

pre-ejaculatory fluid—a clear, alkaline fluid, secreted by the Cowper's glands, that appears at the tip of the penis before a man ejaculates; a.k.a. "pre-cum"

prepuce—*see* foreskin

prostate—in the male, a gland located under the bladder and behind the pubic bone, just above the perineum, that secretes some of the milky, alkaline fluid contained in semen

prostate-triggered orgasm—a climax attained through stimulation of the prostate

P-spot—*see* perineum

pubococcygeus muscle (PC muscle)—a collective term for the group of pelvic-floor muscles that extend from the pubic bone around both sides of the sex organs and back to the tailbone

pudendum—another term for "vulva"

raphe—the blood-vessel-like seam on the underside of the penis

rectum—the lower part of the large intestine

reflexology—a practice based on the premise that all of the body's organs have reflex points located on other body parts such as the hands and feet; stimulation of the reflex points benefits the corresponding organs

rimming—*see* analingus

root—the part of the penis that attaches to the body

R-spot—*see* raphe

sacrum—the large, triangular bone at the base of the spine

safer sex—vaginal, anal, or oral sex involving practices that reduce the risk of pregnancy, HIV, and STDs

scrotum—the pouch of skin containing numerous sebaceous glands and covered in hair that houses the testicles

semen—the sperm-containing fluid that is ejaculated from the penis

sex toy—an object used to enhance sexual activity

sexual intercourse—sexual activity in which the penis is inserted into the vagina; for some, it is defined as a sexual activity in which the penis is inserted into the anus or in which fingers or a sex toy are inserted into the vagina or anus

sexually transmitted disease (STD)—any disease that can be transmitted via sexual contact

sexually transmitted infection (STI)—*see* sexually transmitted disease

shaft—in the male, the part of the penis that runs between the glans and root; in the female, the part of the clitoris that disappears into the body beneath the clitoral hood

sixty-nine—a sexual position that allows for partners to orally stimulate each other's genitals at the same time

soixante-neuf—French for "sixty-nine"; *see* sixty-nine

sperm—the mature male reproductive cell, which is capable of fertilizing an egg

spontaneous orgasm—an orgasm without any genital contact; a.k.a. "extra-genital orgasm"

sushumna—the fiery central energy meridian, or pathway, that runs up and down the spine

tantra—rituals and practices that were outlined in Hindu and Buddhist scriptures, many of which have been recommended for better sex and relationships, e.g., meditation

testes—the male gonads; a pair of oval-shaped glands housed in the scrotum that manufacture sperm and sex hormones, primarily testosterone; a.k.a. "testicles"

testicle—a testis

Transverse Bones—two acupoints located on the upper border of the pubic bone, each half a finger-width from the midline on either side

urethral opening—the opening through which urine exits the body (and semen in the male); in the female, it is a small, acorn-shaped protrusion located between the clitoris and vaginal opening; in the male, it is a tiny opening located at the tip of the penis

urethral sponge—in the female, spongy erectile tissue that contains the paraurethral glands and ducts; a.k.a. "G-spot"

U-spot—*see* urethral opening

uterine orgasm—*see* vaginal orgasm

uterus—(a.k.a. "womb") a hollow, muscular organ located in the woman's abdomen that houses a fetus during pregnancy

vagina—in the female, a highly muscular, three- to four-inch-long, tube-shaped organ that is penetrated during sexual intercourse and through which a baby passes during birth

vaginal opening—the entrance leading from the outside into the female's vagina, through which a baby passes during birth and through which menstrual blood passes during a woman's period

vaginal orgasm—climax emanating from anywhere in the vaginal canal, often the G-spot

vibrator—a battery-operated or plug-in electrical device that vibrates to stimulate body parts, particularly the genitals

vulva—a collective term for the female external genitals, including the mons pubis, clitoris, labia minora, labia majora, urethral opening, and vaginal opening

vulval/vulvic orgasm—a climax attained from the stimulation of a woman's genitals

V-zone—the erogenous area on the lower abdomen stretching from each hipbone to the groin

wet dream—*see* nocturnal orgasm

X-spot—*see* cervix

yoga—a Hindu theistic philosophy and system of exercises teaching the suppression and/or control of all bodily or mental activity for liberation and improved well-being

Resources and Recommended Reading

Acupressure

Acupressure for Lovers, by Dr. Michael Reed Gach (New York: Bantam Books, 1997).

The Complete Idiot's Guide to Acupuncture and Acupressure, by David W. Sollars (New York: Penguin Books, 2000).

Anal Sex

Anal Sex for Couples: A Guaranteed Guide for Painless Pleasure, by Bill Strong and Lori E. Gammon (Zion, IL: Triad Press, Inc., 2006).

The Ultimate Guide to Anal Sex for Men, by Bill Brent (San Francisco, CA: Cleis Press, 2002).

The Ultimate Guide to Anal Sex for Women, 2nd ed., by Tristan Taormino (San Francisco, CA: Cleis Press, 2006).

Female Ejaculation

The Case of the Female Orgasm: Bias in the Science of Evolution, by Elisabeth A. Lloyd (Harvard University Press, 2005).

Female Ejaculation and the G-Spot, by Deborah Sundahl (Alameda, CA: Hunter House, 2003).

G-Spot

The Good Vibrations Guide: The G-Spot, by Cathy Winks (San Francisco, CA: Down There Press, 1998).

The G-Spot and Other Discoveries about Human Sexuality, by Beverly Whipple, John D. Perry, and Alice Khan Ladas (New York: Owl Books, 2004).

Operation G-spot, by Jodi Lynn Copeland (New York: Aphrodisia, 2006).

Orgasms: How to Have Them, Give Them, and Keep Them Coming, 2nd ed., by Lou Paget (New York: Broadway, 2004).

Unleashing Her G-spot Orgasm: A Step-by-Step Guide to Giving a Woman Ultimate Sexual Ecstasy, by Donald L. Hicks (Berkeley, CA: Amorata Press, 2006).

Masturbation

Masturbation as a Means of Achieving Sexual Health, by Walter O. Bockting and Eli Coleman (Binghamton, NY: Haworth Press, 2003).

Sex for One, by Betty Dodson (New York: Harmony Books, 1996).

Jackin World website, www.jackinworld.com (focuses on male masturbation)

Viva La Vulva: Women's Sex Organs Revealed, by Betty Dodson (video of group seminar teaching women to reclaim their bodies and pleasure themselves; available through www.bettydodson.com, or call 866-877-9676).

Reflexology

Reflexology: Health at Your Fingertips, by Barbara and Kevin Kunz (New York: DK Publishing, 2003).

Sexual Reflexology, by Mantak Chia and William U. Wei (Rochester, VT: Destiny Books, 2003).

Sex Education and Information

The Naked Truth about Sex: A Guide to Intelligent Sexual Choices for Teenagers & Twentysomethings, by Roger W. Libby (Topanga, CA: Freedom Press, 2006).

Go Ask Alice!, www.goaskalice.columbia.edu (Columbia University's Health Education Program; Q&A site)

San Francisco Sex Information, www.sfsi.org, or call (415) 989-7374 or (877) 472-SFSI (7374). Answers frequently asked questions, posts a weekly column, and provides referrals.

Sexuality Information and Education Council of the United States, www.siecus.org, (212) 819-0109. Nonprofit organization providing sex education programs and materials.

Sexuality Source, Inc., www.sexualitysource.com (or www.yvonnekfulbright.com). Offers sex education and consulting services, including a free newsletter. Is affiliated with www.sensualfusion.com.

Society for Human Sexuality, www.sexuality.org. Features information and articles on a variety of sex topics, as well as book, video, and product reviews.

Spanish-language sexuality website, www.gentejoven.org.mx.

Sex Toys/Sexual Enhancements

Em & Lo's Sex Toys: An A-Z Guide to Bedside Accessories, by Em & Lo & Arthur Mount (San Francisco, CA: Chronicle Books, 2006).

The Many Joys of Sex Toys: The Ultimate How to Handbook for Couples and Singles by Anne Semans (New York: Broadway, 2004).

(Internet sources for sexual enhancers, books, videos, and safer sex supplies.)

Sexuality Source Enhancements Store, www.sexualitysource.com

Adam and Eve, www.adameve.com
Condomania, www.condomania.com
Eve's Garden, www.evesgarden.com
Good Vibrations (catalogs), www.goodvibes.com
Toys in Babeland, www.babeland.com

Sexual Health

The Hot Guide to Safer Sex, by Yvonne K. Fulbright (Alameda, CA: Hunter House, 2003).

The Lesbian Health Book: Caring for Ourselves, by Jocelyn White and Marissa C. Martinez (Emeryville, CA: Seal Press, 1997).

Love in the Time of HIV: The Gay Man's Guide to Sex, Dating & Relationships, by Michael Mancilla and Lisa Troshinsky (New York: The Guilford Press, 2003).

Safe Sex 101: An Overview for Teens, by Margaret O. Hyde and Elizabeth H. Forsyth (Breckenridge, CO: Twenty-First Century Books, 2006).

Sexual Health for Men, by Richard F. Spark (Jackson, TN: Perseus Books, 2000).

A Woman's Guide to Sexual Health, by Mary Jane Minkin & Carol V. Wright (Yale Univ. Press, 2004).

Sexual Health Network, www.sexualhealth.com (provides sexuality information, education, and other resources)

The Women's Sexual Health Foundation, www.twshf.org

World Association for Sexual Health, www.worldsexology.org

Sexual Pleasuring

The Big O, 2nd ed., by Lou Paget (London: Piatkus Books, 2002).

The Clitoral Truth: The Secret World at Your Fingertips, by Rebecca Chalker (New York: Seven Stories Press, 2000).

The Complete Manual of Sexual Positions, by Jessica Stewart (Chatsworth, CA: Sexual Enrichment Series, 1983).

The Complete Idiot's Guide to Sensual Massage, by Patti Britton (Royersford, PA: Alpha, 2003).

Fearless Sex, by Joy Davidson (Gloucester, MA: Fair Winds Press, 2004).

The Great Lover Playbook: 365 Sexual Tips & Techniques to Keep the Fires Burning All Year Long, by Lou Paget (New York: Gotham, 2005).

How to Be a Great Lover: Girlfriend-to-Girlfriend Totally Explicit Techniques that Will Blow His Mind, by Lou Paget (New York: Broadway, 1999).

How to Be a Great Lover, by Lou Paget (London: Piatkus Books, 2000).

How to Give Her Absolute Pleasure, by Lou Paget (London: Piatkus Books, 2002).

Sexual Pleasure, 2nd ed., by Barbara Keesling (Alameda, CA: Hunter House, 2005).

Taboo: Forbidden Fantasies for Couples, by Violet Blue (San Francisco, CA: Cleis Press, 2004).

365 Days of Sensational Sex, by Lou Paget (London: Hodder Mobius, 2004).

Human Sexuality, Inc., www.howtohavegoodsex.com

Tantric Sex

The Art of Sexual Ecstasy, by Margo Anand (New York: Putnam Books, 1989).

The Art of Tantric Sex, by Nitya Lacroix (New York: DK Publishing, 1997).

The Complete Idiot's Guide to Tantric Sex, 2nd ed., by Judy Kuriansky (New York: Alpha Books, 2004).

Tantric Love, by Ma Ananda Sarita and Swami Anand Geho (London: Gaia Books, 2001).

Tantric Sex for Women, by Christa Schulte (Alameda, CA: Hunter House, 2005).

Yoga

The Art of Sensual Yoga, by Robert Kirby, Connie Dunne Kirby, and Geraldine Ross (New York: Plume, 1997).

Lovers' Yoga: Soothing Stretches for Two, by Darrin Zeer and Thorina Rose (San Francisco, CA: Chronicle, 2005).

Om Yoga in a Box for Couples (available at www.yoga.com).

Sexy Yoga, by Ellen Barrett (Berkeley, CA: Ulysses Press, 2005).

Yoga Journal magazine, www.yogajournal.com

Index

temples, 22, 114, 117
Testicle Breathing, 98
testicles (gonads), 7, 14, 69, 75–76,
    86, 95–102, 133, 144, 160, 180,
    195, 199
thighs, 26, 54, 67, 147–148, 160
third eye, 6, 8, 59, 115, 117, 125,
    170
throat, 8, 78, 91, 117, 119
throat chakra, 6, 8, 119, 167, 170,
    175
thumb walking, 13, 168, 175
thyroid, 8, 119, 139, 167, 170, 175
titty fucking, 79, 108
tongue, 131–132
Transverse Bone, 29–30, 79–80, 189,
    194, 200
treasure trail, 145

U
upper-back points, 141–142
Upward Dog (Urdhva Muhka
    Svanasana), 31, 164
Urdhva Muhka Svanasana. *See* Up-
    ward Dog
urethra, 14, 16, 18, 34–36, 45, 56,
    69, 84
urethral opening, 20, 48, 52–53, 68
urethral sponge, 34, 38, 45, 52
U-spot, 52–53, 68. *See also* urethral
    opening
Ustrasana, 81, 165. *See* Camel Pose
uterus, 35, 37, 58, 133, 144, 169–
    170, 176

V
vagina, 16, 23, 27–28, 30–31, 34–35,
    37–38, 40–41, 44–45, 48–50, 53–
    59, 71, 84, 90, 139, 159, 178, 189–
    190, 199; sex toys and, 184–185;
    sexual health and, 189
vaginal lips, 17, 24, 26, 51. *See also*
    inner lips and outer lips
vaginal opening, 16–17, 40, 48, 52–
    55, 91, 160–161, 181
Virasana. *See* Hero's Pose
V-zone, 145

W
Water Rushing, 119
Wei, William, 98
Whipple, Beverly, 36, 46
Wind Mansion, 116–117
Womb and Vitals, 29, 144, 199
wrist, 21, 138, 151, 168–171

X
X-spot. *See* cervix

Y
Yin-Chio, 146
Yui-Gen (medulla), 116
yoga, *xviii*, 1, 5, 10, 14
yoga poses, 30–32, 60–61, 81–82,
    100–102, 110, 149–151, 163–165
Yung Chuan. *See* Bubbling Spring

Z
Zaviacic, Milan, 46

Printed in the USA
CPSIA information can be obtained
at www.ICGtesting.com
JSHW082200140824
68134JS00014B/338